"BE MUCH OCCUPIED
― WITH ―
JESUS"

SEA HARP PRESS

Other Books by Sea Harp Press

Called to the Wild
Christopher Lawrence

Looking for the One
David McIver

**Discover a faith
that is costly, rich,
alive & true**

Finding the Kingdom

© Copyright 2023 – Finding the Kingdom by C. S. Lewis, Augustine of Hippo, Charles H. Spurgeon, A.W. Tozer, G. K. Chesterton, Athanasius of Alexandria, John Calvin, George MacDonald, Andrew Murray, J. B. Phillips, Alfred Eldersheim,

Compiled by Eugene Luning

This edition copyright © 2023 — Sea Harp
An imprint of Nori Media Group
P.O. Box 310, Shippensburg, PA 17257-0310
"Be Much Occupied with Jesus"

Cover design and interior page design copyright 2022.

All rights reserved.

Cover design by Christian Rafetto

All rights reserved. This book is protected by the copyright laws of the United States of America. This book may not be copied or reprinted for commercial gain or profit. The use of short quotations or occasional page copying for personal or group study is permitted and encouraged. Permission will be granted upon request. Unless otherwise identified Scripture quotations are taken from the King James Version. Scripture quotations marked Phillips are taken from The New Testament in Modern English by J.B Phillips copyright © 1960, 1972 J. B. Phillips. Administered by The Archbishops' Council of the Church of England. Used by Permission.

This book and all other Sea Harp books are available at Christian bookstores and distributors worldwide.

For more information on foreign distributors, call 717-532-3040.

Reach us on the Internet: www.seaharp.com

ISBN 13 TP: 978-0-7684-7499-2

ISBN 13 eBook: 978-0-7684-7500-5

For Worldwide Distribution, Printed in the U.S.A.

1 2 3 4 5 6 7 8 / 27 26 25 24 23

Contents

Foreword 6

Introduction 8

Encountering God in Jesus 11

Coming to Know the Personality & Power of God in Jesus 21

Hearing and Following the Words of Jesus 32

The Cross of Jesus 40

The Resurrection of Jesus 50

The Ascension of Jesus 60

Learning to Approach the Throne of Grace with Confidence 68

The Holy Spirit of Jesus 76

Extending the Realm of the Kingdom of Heaven 84

Afterword 94

Foreword

WHEN WE FOUNDED SEA HARP PRESS, it was with one overarching aim: in the words of Andrew Murray, to "be much occupied with Jesus, and believe much in Him, as the True Vine." We desire to reinvigorate the Church's reading of the best of the past, to bring out fresh editions of both today's and tomorrow's classics, all for the purpose of personal encounter with Jesus Himself. In fact, for every author, post, podcast, artwork or book we consider publishing, we ask ourselves two fundamental questions:

Is this work entirely about the person of Jesus of Nazareth?

Would the Early Church have thought this work worthy of passing around?

As we first got going, I kept asking my cofounder, Christian Rafetto, the same question over and over again: *As we read through the Gospels and Acts, doesn't it become clearer and clearer that Jesus' pattern with His original disciples might, in fact, be THE pattern He still wants for us, His Body?*

Think about it: He began with direct personal encounter: *"Follow Me"*... then His disciples came to know and enjoy His person and personality... then, for three years, they heard His every word, learned to listen and obey His teachings... then, upon the Cross, He "finished" the work—made His children holy and blameless... then, on the morning of Easter, He ended death for all who'd believe in Him... then, with His Ascension, He returned—*as a Man*—to the throne of Heaven... and, from there, He invited His friends to approach the throne of grace with confidence... then He sent His very own Spirit to inhabit His followers' hearts... and then He delighted to watch His men and women bring the Kingdom of Heaven unto all.

So, here's our beating heart for you, our young adult friends all over the country:

- That you would have direct personal encounter with Jesus.
- That you would come to know His personality for yourself.
- That you would hear His words, and learn to listen and obey the actual things He actually asked His people to do.
- That you would learn to live as the faultless, flawless children of the Cross.
- That you would, like the Early Church, become fearless acolytes of the power of the Resurrection.
- That you would know the glory of our Friend, our Savior, reigning in Heaven on our behalf.
- That you would learn to approach the throne of grace with greater confidence.
- That you would fall in love with the Holy Spirit, sent personally to us.
- That you would carry Jesus and His Kingdom of Heaven unto all. Every day.

We hope this simple work, a compilation of some of the greatest voices of the Church's past, will be a blessing to your journey along the Way. And we want you to hear this: *we believe in you.* We believe your generation will carry great power in the economy of the Kingdom of Heaven. We already see you doing so.

His friend and yours,

Eugene Luning

Cofounder

Sea Harp Press

Introduction

C.S. Lewis

1942

EVERY AGE has its own outlook. It is specially good at seeing certain truths and specially liable to make certain mistakes. We all, therefore, need the books that will correct the characteristic mistakes of our own period. And that means the old books. All contemporary writers share to some extent the contemporary outlook—even those, like myself, who seem most opposed to it. Nothing strikes me more when I read the controversies of past ages than the fact that both sides were usually assuming without question a good deal which we should now absolutely deny. They thought that they were as completely opposed as two sides could be, but in fact they were all the time secretly united— united with each other and against earlier and later ages—by a great mass of common assumptions. We may be sure that the characteristic blindness of the twentieth century—the blindness about which posterity will ask, "But how could they have thought that?"—lies where we have never suspected it, and concerns something about which there is untroubled agreement between Hitler and President Roosevelt or between Mr. H. G. Wells and Karl Barth. None of us can fully escape this blindness, but we shall certainly increase it, and weaken our guard against it, if we read only modern books. Where they are true they will give us truths which we half knew already. Where they are false they will aggravate the error with which we are already dangerously ill. The only palliative is to keep the clean sea breeze of the centuries blowing through our minds, and this can be done only by reading old books. Not, of course, that there is any magic about the past. People were no cleverer then than they are now; they made as many mistakes as we. But not the same mistakes. They will not flatter us in the errors we are already committing; and their own errors, being now open and palpable, will not endanger us. Two heads are better than one, not because either is infallible, but because they are unlikely to go wrong in the same direction. To be sure, the books of the future would be just as good a corrective as the books of the past, but unfortunately we cannot get at them.

I myself was first led into reading the Christian classics, almost accidentally, as a result of my English studies. Some, such as Hooker, Herbert, Traherne, Taylor and Bunyan, I read because they are themselves great English writers; others, such as Boethius, St. Augustine, Thomas Aquinas and, Dante, because they were "influences." George Macdonald I had found for myself at the age of sixteen and never wavered in my allegiance, though I tried for a long time to ignore his Christianity. They are, you will note, a mixed bag, representative of many Churches, climates and ages. And that brings me to yet another reason for reading them. The divisions of Christendom are undeniable and are by some of these writers most fiercely expressed. But if any man is tempted to think—as one might be tempted who read only contemporaries—that "Christianity" is a word of so many meanings that it means nothing at all, he can learn beyond all doubt, by stepping out of his own century, that this is not so. Measured against the ages "mere Christianity" turns out to be no insipid interdenominational transparency, but something positive, self-consistent, and inexhaustible. I know it, indeed, to my cost. In the days when I still hated Christianity, I learned to recognise, like some all too familiar smell, that almost unvarying something which met me, now in Puritan Bunyan, now in Anglican Hooker, now in Thomist Dante. It was there (honeyed and floral) in Francois de Sales; it was there (grave and homely) in Spenser and Walton; it was there (grim but manful) in Pascal and Johnson; there again, with a mild, frightening, Paradisial flavour, in Vaughan and Boehme and Traherne. In the urban sobriety of the eighteenth century one was not safe—Law and Butler were two lions in the path. The supposed "Paganism" of the Elizabethans could not keep it out; it lay in wait where a man might have supposed himself safest, in the very centre of *The Faerie Queene* and the *Arcadia*. It was, of course, varied; and yet—after all—so unmistakably the same; recognisable, not to be evaded, the odour which is death to us until we allow it to become life:

> ...an air that kills
> From yon far country blows.

We are all rightly distressed, and ashamed also, at the divisions of Christendom. But those who have always lived within the Christian fold may be too easily dispirited by them. They are bad, but such people do not know what it looks like from without. Seen from there, what is left intact despite all the divisions, still appears (as it truly is) an immensely formidable unity. I know, for I saw it; and well our enemies know it. That unity any of us can find by going out of his own age. It is not enough, but it is more than you had thought till then. Once you are well soaked in it, if you then venture to speak, you will have an amusing experience. You will be thought a Papist when you are actually reproducing Bunyan, a Pantheist when you are quoting Aquinas, and so forth. For you have now got on to the great level viaduct which crosses the ages and which looks so high from the valleys, so low from the mountains, so narrow compared with the swamps, and so broad compared with the sheep-tracks....

C.S. Lewis
Oxford, England

Encountering God in Jesus

Love, Self-Revealed

Athanasius of Alexandria
4th Century, A.D.

BECAUSE DEATH AND CORRUPTION were gaining ever firmer hold on them, the human race was in process of destruction. Man, who was created in God's image and in his possession of reason reflected the very Word Himself, was disappearing, and the work of God was being undone. The law of death, which followed from the Transgression, prevailed upon us, and from it there was no escape. The thing that was happening was in truth both monstrous and unfitting. It would, of course, have been unthinkable that God should go back upon His word and that man, having transgressed, should not die; but it was equally monstrous that beings which once had shared the nature of the Word should perish and turn back again into non-existence through corruption. It was unworthy of the goodness of God that creatures made by Him should be brought to nothing through the deceit wrought upon man by the devil; and it was supremely unfitting that the work of God in mankind should disappear, either through their own negligence or through the deceit of evil spirits. As, then, the creatures whom He had created reasonable, like the Word, were in fact perishing, and such noble works were on the road to ruin, what then was God, being Good, to do? Was He to let corruption and death have their way with them? In that case, what was the use of having made them in the beginning? Surely it would have been better never to have been created at all than, having been created, to be neglected and perish; and, besides that, such indifference to the ruin of His own work before His very eyes would argue not goodness in God but limitation, and that far more than if He had never created men at all. It was impossible, therefore, that God should leave man to be carried off by corruption, because it would be unfitting and unworthy of Himself.

Yet, true though this is, it is not the whole matter. As we have already noted, it was unthinkable that God, the Father of Truth, should go back upon His word regarding death in order to ensure our continued existence. He could not falsify Himself; what, then, was God to do? Was He to demand repentance from men for their transgression? You might say that that was worthy of God, and argue further that, as through the Transgression they became subject to corruption, so through repentance they might return to incorruption again. But repentance would not guard the Divine consistency, for, if death did not hold dominion over men, God would still remain untrue. Nor does repentance recall men from what is according to their nature; all that it does is to make them cease from sinning. Had it been a case of a trespass only, and not of a subsequent corruption, repentance would have been well enough; but when once transgression had begun men came under the power of the corruption proper to their nature and were bereft of the grace which belonged to them as creatures in the Image of God. No, repentance could not meet the case. What—or rather Who—was it that was needed for such grace and such recall as we required? Who, save the Word of God Himself, Who also in the beginning had made all things out of nothing? His part it was, and His alone, both to bring again the corruptible to incorruption and to maintain for the Father His consistency of character with all. For He alone, being Word of the Father and above all, was in consequence both able to recreate all, and worthy to suffer on behalf of all and to be an ambassador for all with the Father.

For this purpose, then, the incorporeal and incorruptible and immaterial Word of God entered our world. In one sense, indeed, He was not far from it before, for no part of creation had ever been without Him Who, while ever abiding in union with the Father, yet fills all things that are. But now He entered the world in a new way, stooping to our level in His love and Self-revealing to us. He saw the reasonable race, the race of men that, like Himself, expressed the Father's Mind, wasting out of existence, and death reigning over all in corruption. He saw that corruption held us all the closer, because it was the penalty for the Transgression; He saw, too, how unthinkable it would be for the law to be repealed before it was fulfilled. He saw how unseemly it was that the very things of which He Himself was the Artificer should be disappearing. He saw how the surpassing wickedness of men was mounting up against them; He saw also their universal liability to death. All this He saw and, pitying our race, moved with compassion for our limitation, unable to endure that death should have the mastery, rather than that His creatures should perish and the work of His Father for us men come to nought, He took to Himself a body, a human body even as our own. Nor did He will merely to become embodied or merely to appear; had that been so, He could have revealed His divine majesty in some other and better way. No, He took our body, and not only so, but He took it directly from a spotless, stainless virgin, without the agency of human father—a pure body, untainted by intercourse with man. He, the Mighty One, the Artificer of all, Himself prepared this body in the virgin as a temple for Himself, and took it for His very own, as the instrument through which He was known and in which He dwelt. Thus, taking a body like our own, because all our bodies were liable to the corruption of death, He surrendered His body to death instead of all, and offered it to the Father. This He did out of sheer love for us, so that in His death all might die, and the law of death thereby be abolished because, having fulfilled in His body that for which it was appointed, it was thereafter voided of its power for men. This He did that He might turn again to incorruption men who had turned back to corruption, and make them alive through death by the appropriation of His body and by the grace of His resurrection. Thus He would make death to disappear from them as utterly as straw from fire.

The Word perceived that corruption could not be got rid of otherwise than through death; yet He Himself, as the Word, being immortal and the Father's Son, was such as could not die. For this reason, therefore, He assumed a body capable of death, in order that it, through belonging to the Word Who is above all, might become in dying a sufficient exchange for all, and, itself remaining incorruptible through His indwelling, might thereafter put an end to corruption for all others as well, by the grace of the resurrection. It was by surrendering to death the body which He had taken, as an offering and sacrifice free from every stain, that He forthwith abolished death for His human brethren by the offering of the equivalent. For naturally, since the Word of God was above all, when He offered His own temple and bodily instrument as a substitute for the life of all, He fulfilled in death all that was required. Naturally also, through this union of the immortal Son of God with our human nature, all men were clothed with incorruption in the promise of the resurrection. For the solidarity of mankind is such that, by virtue of the Word's indwelling in a single human body, the corruption which goes with death has lost its power over all. You know how it is when some great king enters a large city and dwells in one of its houses; because of his dwelling in that single house, the whole city is honoured, and enemies and robbers cease to molest it. Even so is it with the King of all; He has come into our country and dwelt in one body amidst the many, and in consequence the designs of the enemy against mankind have been foiled, and the corruption of death, which formerly held them in its power, has simply ceased to be. For the human race would have perished utterly had not the Lord and Saviour of all, the Son of God, come among us to put an end to death.

This great work was, indeed, supremely worthy of the goodness of God. A king who has founded a city, so far from neglecting it when through the carelessness of the inhabitants it is attacked by robbers, avenges it and saves it from destruction, having regard rather to his own honour than to the people's neglect. Much more, then, the Word of the All-good Father was not unmindful of the human race that He had called to be; but rather, by the offering of His own body He abolished the death which they had incurred, and corrected their neglect by His own teaching. Thus by His own power He restored the whole nature of man. The Saviour's own inspired disciples assure us of this. We read in one place: "For the love of Christ constraineth us, because we thus judge that, if One died on behalf of all, then all died, and He died for all that we should no longer live unto ourselves, but unto Him who died and rose again from the dead, even our Lord Jesus Christ." (2 Corinthians 5:14 f.) And again another says: "But we behold Him Who hath been made a little lower than the angels, even Jesus, because of the suffering of death crowned with glory and honour, that by the grace of God He should taste of death on behalf of every man." The same writer goes on to point out why it was necessary for God the Word and none other to become Man: "For it became Him, for Whom are all things and through Whom are all things, in bringing many sons unto glory, to make the Author of their salvation perfect through suffering." (Hebrews 2:9 ff.) He means that the rescue of mankind from corruption was the proper part only of Him Who made them in the beginning. He points out also that the Word assumed a human body, expressly in order that He might offer it in sacrifice for other like bodies: "Since then the children are sharers in flesh and blood, He also Himself assumed the same, in order that through death He might bring to nought him that bath the power of death, that is to say, the Devil, and might rescue those who all their lives were enslaved by the fear of death." (Hebrews 2:14 f.) For by the sacrifice of His own body He did two things: He put an end to the law of death which barred our way; and He made a new beginning of life for us, by giving us the hope of resurrection. By man death has gained its power over men; by the Word-made-Man death has been destroyed and life raised up anew. That is what Paul says, that true servant of Christ: "For since by man came death, by man came also the resurrection of the dead. Just as in Adam all die, even so in Christ shall all be made alive," (1 Corinthians 15:21 f.) and so forth. Now, therefore, when we die we no longer do so as men condemned to death, but as those who are even now in process of rising; we await the general resurrection of all, "which in its own times He shall show," (1 Timothy 6:15) even God Who wrought it and bestowed it on us.

This, then, is the first cause of the Saviour's becoming Man. There are, however, other things which show how wholly fitting is His blessed presence in our midst; and these we must now go on to consider.

Athanasius of Alexandria
On the Incarnation

> *God has by his own action given us everything that is necessary for living the truly good life, in allowing us to know the one who has called us to him, through his own glorious goodness. It is through him that God's greatest and most precious promises have become available to us men.*
>
> 2 Peter 1:3,4a, Phillips

"A spiritual kingdom lies all about us, enclosing us, embracing us, altogether within reach of our inner selves, waiting for us to recognize it. God Himself is here waiting our response to His Presence. This eternal world will come alive to us the moment we begin to reckon upon its reality."

A.W. Tozer
The Pursuit of God

"This is the way, dear friends, in which we found our salvation, Jesus Christ, the high priest of our offerings, the protector and helper of our weakness. Through him we fix our gaze on the heights of heaven. In him we see mirrored God's pure and transcendent face. Through him the eyes of our hearts have been opened. Through him our foolish and darkened understanding springs up to the light. Through him the Master has willed that we should taste immortal knowledge."

Clement of Rome
Epistle to the Corinthians

"God appointed Jesus as a Saviour, not only because He should bring redemption nigh by a sacrifice which He alone could offer, but because He was also appointed to be the firstborn of many brethren; to be the head of a new family, the beginning—the new Adam—the first of a new line, in which character should cease to be merely human, even though perfect with all human perfections, and should become a union of the human and the Divine; in which the body and mind and spirit of man should continue to exhibit the wonder of Christ's Incarnation, and show forth God clothed with man."

Bramwell Booth
Our Master

"O Jesus, Wisdom of God, Eternal Truth, how brightly hath Thy divine light shone down on the sons of Adam! How hath all Thy life, and every action of Thine, been to us, as it were, a light leading us on to the truth! How clearly hath the light of Thy heavenly teaching lit up the darkness! How full were all Thy works of lowliness; and long-suffering, and love, and self-denial; in a word, of every grace and virtue, so that in these were reflected the most perfect examples of all holiness! Therefore, whatever is wanting to me, from these sources will I draw it. If in anything I shall happen to doubt, in Thy holy life as in a clear mirror will I look. For here I find rigorous self-denial, true obedience, profound humility, voluntary poverty, unutterable purity, marvellous patience, unchanging long-suffering, constant perseverance, and incomprehensible charity. Here, also, I find in all abundance, that of which we chiefly stand in need, infinite loving-kindness and mercy,—yea, and all the virtues that I can possibly think of in my heart, all these I clearly discover written down as on a tablet. Of a truth, Thou art that book which the prophet saw written within and without, for all Thy life, both outward and inward, is full of spiritual teaching, and all virtue."

Johannes Tauler
Meditations on the Life and Passion of our Lord Jesus Christ

"But there is a place at which God and the cosmic reality are reconciled, a place at which God and man have become one. That and that alone is what enables man to set his eyes upon God and upon the world at the same time. This place does not lie somewhere out beyond reality in the realm of ideas. It lies in the midst of history as a divine miracle. It lies in Jesus Christ, the Reconciler of the world."

Dietrich Bonhoeffer
Ethics

"I am persuaded that there is no great actual distance between earth and heaven: the distance lies in our dull minds. When the Beloved visits us in the night, He makes our chambers to be the vestibule of His palace-halls. Earth rises to heaven when heaven comes down to earth...."

Charles Spurgeon
Till He Come

'Tis So Sweet to Trust in Jesus

1
'Tis so sweet to trust in Jesus,
Just to take Him at His Word;
Just to rest upon His promise;
Just to know, "Thus saith the Lord."

Chorus:
Jesus, Jesus, how I trust Him!
How I've prov'd Him o'er and o'er!
Jesus, Jesus, Precious Jesus!
O for grace to trust Him more!

2
O how sweet to trust in Jesus,
Just to trust His cleansing blood;
Just in simple faith to plunge me
'Neath the healing, cleansing flood! [Chorus]

3
Yes, 'tis sweet to trust in Jesus,
Just from sin and self to cease;
Just from Jesus simply taking
Life, and rest, and joy, and peace. [Chorus]

4
I'm so glad I learned to trust Thee,
Precious Jesus, Savior, Friend;
And I know that Thou art with me,
Wilt be with me to the end. [Chorus]

Louisa M.R. Stead

A Prayer

Jesus, I've hardly begun to know you yet—but that's what I want: To encounter you, to experience the wonder of your presence, to be swept off my feet at your invitation to follow alongside you. Please come and encounter me in fresh ways every day. My heart and eyes are open to see you.

Thank you that you showed up in the first place. I long to know you more and more and more, every day.

In your name, Jesus.

Amen.

Coming to Know the Personality & Power of God in Jesus

Following Hard after God

A.W. Tozer
1948

"My soul followeth hard after thee: thy right hand upholdeth me."

—Psalm 63:8

CHRISTIAN THEOLOGY TEACHES the doctrine of prevenient grace, which briefly stated means this, that before a man can seek God, God must first have sought the man.

Before a sinful man can think a right thought of God, there must have been a work of enlightenment done within him; imperfect it may be, but a true work nonetheless, and the secret cause of all desiring and seeking and praying which may follow.

We pursue God because, and only because, He has first put an urge within us that spurs us to the pursuit. "No man can come to me," said our Lord, "except the Father which hath sent me draw him," and it is by this very prevenient *drawing* that God takes from us every vestige of credit for the act of coming. The impulse to pursue God originates with God, but the outworking of that impulse is our following hard after Him; and all the time we are pursuing Him we are already in His hand: "Thy right hand upholdeth me."

In this divine "upholding" and human "following" there is no contradiction. All is of God, for as von Hügel teaches, *God is always previous*. In practice, however, (that is, where God's previous working meets man's present response) man must pursue God. On our part there must be positive reciprocation if this secret drawing of God is to eventuate in identifiable experience of the Divine. In the warm language of personal feeling this is stated in the Forty-second Psalm: "As the hart panteth after the water brooks, so panteth my soul after thee, O God. My soul thirsteth for God, for the living God: when shall I come and appear before God?" This is deep calling unto deep, and the longing heart will understand it.

The doctrine of justification by faith—a Biblical truth, and a blessed relief from sterile legalism and unavailing self-effort—has in our time fallen into evil company and been interpreted by many in such manner as actually to bar men from the knowledge of God. The whole transaction of religious conversion has been made mechanical and spiritless. Faith may now be exercised without a jar to the moral life and without embarrassment to the Adamic[1] ego. Christ may be "received" without creating any special love for Him in the soul of the receiver. The man is "saved," but he is not hungry nor thirsty after God. In fact he is specifically taught to be satisfied and encouraged to be content with little.

The modern scientist has lost God amid the wonders of His world; we Christians are in real danger of losing God amid the wonders of His Word. We have almost forgotten that God is a Person and, as such, can be cultivated as any person can. It is inherent in personality to be able to know other personalities, but full knowledge of one personality by another cannot be achieved in one encounter. It is only after long and loving mental intercourse that the full possibilities of both can be explored.

All social intercourse between human beings is a response of personality to personality, grading upward from the most casual brush between man and man to the fullest, most intimate communion of which the human soul is capable. Religion, so far as it is genuine, is in essence the response of created personalities to the Creating Personality, God. "This is life eternal, that they might know thee the only true God, and Jesus Christ, whom thou hast sent."

God is a Person, and in the deep of His mighty nature He thinks, wills, enjoys, feels, loves, desires and suffers as any other person may. In making Himself known to us He stays by the familiar pattern of personality. He communicates with us through the avenues of our minds, our wills and our emotions. The continuous and unembarrassed interchange of love and thought between God and the soul of the redeemed man is the throbbing heart of New Testament religion.

---

[1] Meaning, "like Adam"

This intercourse between God and the soul is known to us in conscious personal awareness. It is personal: that is, it does not come through the body of believers, as such, but is known to the individual, and to the body through the individuals which compose it. And it is conscious: that is, it does not stay below the threshold of consciousness and work there unknown to the soul (as, for instance, infant baptism is thought by some to do), but comes within the field of awareness where the man can "know" it as he knows any other fact of experience.

You and I are in little (our sins excepted) what God is in large. Being made in His image we have within us the capacity to know Him. In our sins we lack only the power. The moment the Spirit has quickened us to life in regeneration our whole being senses its kinship to God and leaps up in joyous recognition. That is the heavenly birth without which we cannot see the Kingdom of God. It is, however, not an end but an inception, for now begins the glorious pursuit, the heart's happy exploration of the infinite riches of the Godhead. That is where we begin, I say, but where we stop no man has yet discovered, for there is in the awful and mysterious depths of the Triune God neither limit nor end.

> Shoreless Ocean, who can sound Thee?
> Thine own eternity is round Thee,
> Majesty divine!

To have found God and still to pursue Him is the soul's paradox of love, scorned indeed by the too-easily-satisfied religionist, but justified in happy experience by the children of the burning heart. St. Bernard stated this holy paradox in a musical quatrain that will be instantly understood by every worshipping soul:

> We taste Thee, O Thou Living Bread,
> And long to feast upon Thee still:
> We drink of Thee, the Fountainhead
> And thirst our souls from Thee to fill.

Come near to the holy men and women of the past and you will soon feel the heat of their desire after God. They mourned for Him, they prayed and wrestled and sought for Him day and night, in season and out, and when they had found Him the finding was all the sweeter for the long seeking. Moses used the fact that he knew God as an argument for knowing Him better. "Now, therefore, I pray thee, if I have found grace in thy sight, show me now thy way, that I may know thee, that I may find grace in thy sight"; and from there he rose to make the daring request, "I beseech thee, show me thy glory." God was frankly pleased by this display of ardor, and the next day called Moses into the mount, and there in solemn procession made all His glory pass before him.

David's life was a torrent of spiritual desire, and his psalms ring with the cry of the seeker and the glad shout of the finder. Paul confessed the mainspring of his life to be his burning desire after Christ. "That I may know Him," was the goal of his heart, and to this he sacrificed everything. "Yea doubtless, and I count all things but loss for the excellency of the knowledge of Christ Jesus my Lord: for whom I have suffered the loss of all things, and do count them but refuse, that I may win Christ."

Hymnody is sweet with the longing after God, the God whom, while the singer seeks, he knows he has already found. "His track I see and I'll pursue," sang our fathers only a short generation ago, but that song is heard no more in the great congregation. How tragic that we in this dark day have had our seeking done for us by our teachers. Everything is made to center upon the initial act of "accepting" Christ (a term, incidentally, which is not found in the Bible) and we are not expected thereafter to crave any further revelation of God to our souls. We have been snared in the coils of a spurious logic which insists that if we have found Him we need no more seek Him. This is set before us as the last word in orthodoxy, and it is taken for granted that no Bible-taught Christian ever believed otherwise. Thus the whole testimony of the worshipping, seeking, singing Church on that subject is crisply set aside. The experiential heart-theology of a grand army of fragrant saints is rejected in favor of a smug interpretation of Scripture which would certainly have sounded strange to an Augustine, a Rutherford or a Brainerd.

In the midst of this great chill there are some, I rejoice to acknowledge, who will not be content with shallow logic. They will admit the force of the argument, and then turn away with tears to hunt some lonely place and pray, "O God, show me thy glory." They want to taste, to touch with their hearts, to see with their inner eyes the wonder that is God.

I want deliberately to encourage this mighty longing after God. The lack of it has brought us to our present low estate. The stiff and wooden quality about our religious lives is a result of our lack of holy desire. Complacency is a deadly foe of all spiritual growth. Acute desire must be present or there will be no manifestation of Christ to His people. He waits to be wanted. Too bad that with many of us He waits so long, so very long, in vain.

Every age has its own characteristics. Right now we are in an age of religious complexity. The simplicity which is in Christ is rarely found among us. In its stead are programs, methods, organizations and a world of nervous activities which occupy time and attention but can never satisfy the longing of the heart. The shallowness of our inner experience, the hollowness of our worship, and that servile imitation of the world which marks our promotional methods all testify that we, in this day, know God only imperfectly, and the peace of God scarcely at all.

If we would find God amid all the religious externals we must first determine to find Him, and then proceed in the way of simplicity. Now as always God discovers Himself to "babes" and hides Himself in thick darkness from the wise and the prudent. We must simplify our approach to Him. We must strip down to essentials (and they will be found to be blessedly few). We must put away all effort to impress, and come with the guileless candor of childhood. If we do this, without doubt God will quickly respond.

When religion has said its last word, there is little that we need other than God Himself. The evil habit of seeking *God-and* effectively prevents us from finding God in full revelation. In the "and" lies our great woe. If we omit the "and" we shall soon find God, and in Him we shall find that for which we have all our lives been secretly longing.

We need not fear that in seeking God only we may narrow our lives or restrict the motions of our expanding hearts. The opposite is true. We can well afford to make God our All, to concentrate, to sacrifice the many for the One.

The author of the quaint old English classic, *The Cloud of Unknowing*, teaches us how to do this. "Lift up thine heart unto God with a meek stirring of love; and mean Himself, and none of His goods. And thereto, look thee loath to think on aught but God Himself. So that nought work in thy wit, nor in thy will, but only God Himself. This is the work of the soul that most pleaseth God."

Again, he recommends that in prayer we practice a further stripping down of everything, even of our theology. "For it sufficeth enough, a naked intent direct unto God without any other cause than Himself." Yet underneath all his thinking lay the broad foundation of New Testament truth, for he explains that by "Himself" he means "God that made thee, and bought thee, and that graciously called thee to thy degree." And he is all for simplicity: If we would have religion "lapped and folden in one word, for that thou shouldst have better hold thereupon, take thee but a little word of one syllable: for so it is better than of two, for even the shorter it is the better it accordeth with the work of the Spirit. And such a word is this word GOD or this word LOVE."

When the Lord divided Canaan among the tribes of Israel Levi received no share of the land. God said to him simply, "I am thy part and thine inheritance," and by those words made him richer than all his brethren, richer than all the kings and rajas who have ever lived in the world. And there is a spiritual principle here, a principle still valid for every priest of the Most High God.

The man who has God for his treasure has all things in One. Many ordinary treasures may be denied him, or if he is allowed to have them, the enjoyment of them will be so tempered that they will never be necessary to his happiness. Or if he must see them go, one after one, he will scarcely feel a sense of loss, for having the Source of all things he has in One all satisfaction, all pleasure, all delight. Whatever he may lose he has actually lost nothing, for he now has it all in One, and he has it purely, legitimately and forever.

A.W. Tozer
The Pursuit of God

We are writing to you about something which has always existed yet which we ourselves actually saw and heard: something which we had an opportunity to observe closely and even to hold in our hands, and yet, as we know now, was something of the very Word of life himself! For it was life which appeared before us: we saw it, we are eye-witnesses of it, and are now writing to you about it. It was the very life of all ages, the life that has always existed with the Father, which actually became visible in person to us mortal men. We repeat, we really saw and heard what we are now writing to you about. We want you to be with us in this—in this fellowship with the Father, and Jesus Christ his Son. We must write and tell you about it, because the more that fellowship extends the greater the joy it brings to us who are already in it.

1 JOHN 1:1-4, Phillips

"Let it be our most earnest study, therefore, to dwell upon the life of Jesus Christ. His teaching surpasseth all teaching of holy men, and such as have His Spirit find therein the hidden manna (Rev. 2:17)."

Thomas à Kempis
The Imitation of Christ

"The task, then, which we have now to perform, is to gather together into a whole the various features of the *portrait of the Lord Jesus*, as furnished by the Gospels. This is a subject which, as all must allow, can never be exhaustively treated,—a task whose accomplishment can at best be but approximated. It is a theme infinite in its nature, and ever offering new aspects, at various ages of the world, and in successive stages of human development."

Carl Ullman
The Sinlessness of Jesus

"Jesus Christ saith, He hath the Life in Himself. All other beings have only a borrowed life; but the Word hath the Life in Himself, and being communicative of His nature He desireth to communicate it to man. We should, therefore, make room for the influx of this Life...."

Madame Guyon
A Method of Prayer

"Do not torture yourself, remember that woman [caught in adultery, in John 8], that there was no one who condemned her, and bear in mind that this same things can be expressed also in another way: Christ was present. Precisely because he was present, there was no one who condemned her. He rescued her from the condemnation of the Pharisees and Scribes; they went away ashamed; because Christ was present, there was no one who condemned her. Then Christ alone remained with her—but there was no one who condemned her. Just this, that he alone remained with her, signifies in a far deeper sense that there was no one who condemned her. It would have been of only little help to her that the Pharisees and Scribes went away; after all, they could come again with their condemnation. But the *Savior* alone remained with her: therefore there was no one who condemned her. Alas, there is only one guilt that God cannot forgive—it is to refuse to believe in his greatness!"

Søren Kierkegaard
Christian Discourses

"Jesus Christ took the place and fulfilled the destiny of man, as a creature, by His life of perfect humility. His humility is our salvation. His salvation is our humility."

Andrew Murray
Humility

"The stories of the friendships of Jesus when he was on the earth need cause no one to sigh, 'I wish that I had lived in those days...that I might have been his friend too...' The friendships of Jesus, whose stories we read in the New Testament, are only patterns of friendships into which we may enter, if we are ready to accept what he offers, and to consecrate our life to faithfulness and love."

J.R. Miller
Personal Friendships of Jesus

Vision

I have not walked on common ground,
Nor drunk of earthly streams;
A shining figure, mailed and crowned,
Moves softly through my dreams.

He makes the air so keen and strange,
The stars so fiercely bright;
The rocks of time, the tides of change,
Are nothing in his sight.

Death lays no shadow on his smile;
Life is a race fore-run;
Look in his face a little while,
And life and death are one.

Marjorie Pickthall

A Prayer

Jesus, I want to know you like your first friends did. I want to experience the joy of your personality and the glory of your power. I want to speak of how you are to others and be confident of who you are—because I truly know you for myself.

Would you please reveal yourself to me in the Gospels, in all of the scriptures, and, by your Spirit, by your very own voice? I want to come to know your heart, firsthand. I want to move from knowing *about* you, Lord, to truly *knowing you*.

That is the cry of my heart today.

In your name, Jesus.

Amen.

Hearing and Following the Words of Jesus

Learning to Obey Him in Everything

George MacDonald
1867

TO THE MAN WHO GIVES HIMSELF to the living Lord, every belief will necessarily come right; the Lord himself will see that his disciple believe aright concerning him. If a man cannot trust him for this, what claim can he make to faith in him? It is because he has little or no faith, that he is left clinging to preposterous and dishonouring ideas, the traditions of men concerning his Father, and neither his teaching nor that of his apostles...

What I insist upon is, that a man's faith shall be in the living, loving, ruling, helping Christ, devoted to us as much as ever he was, and with all the powers of the Godhead for the salvation of his brethren. It is not faith that he "did this," that his work "wrought that"—it is faith in the man who did and is doing everything for us that will save him: without this he cannot work to heal spiritually, any more than he would heal physically, when he was present to the eyes of men. Do you ask, 'What is faith in him?' I answer, The leaving of your way, your objects, your self, and the taking of his and him; the leaving of your trust in men, in money, in opinion, in character, in atonement itself, *and doing as he tells you*. I can find no words strong enough to serve for the weight of this necessity—this obedience. It is the one terrible heresy of the church, that it has always been presenting something else than obedience as faith in Christ. The work of Christ is not the Working Christ, any more than the clothing of Christ is the body of Christ. If the woman who touched the hem of his garment had trusted in the garment and not in him who wore it, would she have been healed? And the reason that so many who believe *about* Christ rather than in him, get the comfort they do, is that, touching thus the mere hem of his garment, they cannot help believing a little in the live man inside the garment. It is not wonderful that such believers should so often be miserable; they lay themselves down to sleep with nothing but the skirt of his robe in their hand—a robe too, I say, that never was his, only by them is supposed his—when they might sleep in peace with the living Lord in their hearts. Instead of so knowing Christ that they have him in them saving them, they lie wasting themselves in soul-sickening self-examination as to whether they are believers, whether they are really trusting in the atonement, whether they are truly sorry for their sins—the way to madness of the brain, and despair of the heart. Some even ponder the imponderable—whether they are of the elect, whether they have an interest in the blood shed for sin, whether theirs is a saving faith—when all the time the man who died for them is waiting to begin to save them from every evil—and first from this self which is consuming them with trouble about its salvation; he will set them free, and take them home to the bosom of the Father—if only they will mind what he says to them—which is the beginning, middle, and end of faith. If, instead of searching into the mysteries of corruption in their own charnel-houses, they would but awake and arise from the dead, and come out into the light which Christ is waiting to give them, he would begin at once to fill them with the fulness of God.

'But I do not know how to awake and arise!'

I will tell you:—Get up, and do something the master tells you; so make yourself his disciple at once. Instead of asking yourself whether you believe or not, ask yourself whether you have this day done one thing because he said, Do it, or once abstained because he said, Do not do it. It is simply absurd to say you believe, or even want to believe in him, if you do not anything he tells you. If you can think of nothing he ever said as having had an atom of influence on your doing or not doing, you have too good ground to consider yourself no disciple of his. Do not, I pray you, worse than waste your time in trying to convince yourself that you are his disciple notwithstanding—that for this reason or that you still have cause to think you believe in him. What though you should succeed in persuading yourself to absolute certainty that you are his disciple, if, after all, he say to you, 'Why did you not do the things I told you? Depart from me; I do not know you!' Instead of trying to persuade yourself, if the thing be true you can make it truer; if it be not true, you can begin at once to make it true, to *be* a disciple of the Living One—by obeying him in the first thing you can think of in which you are not obeying him. We must learn to obey him in everything, and so must begin somewhere: let it be at once, and in the very next thing that lies at the door of our conscience! ...

What have you done this day because it was the will of Christ? Have you dismissed, once dismissed, an anxious thought for the morrow? Have you ministered to any needy soul or body, and kept your right hand from knowing what your left hand did? Have you begun to leave all and follow him? Did you set yourself to judge righteous judgment? Are you being wary of covetousness? Have you forgiven your enemy? Are you seeking the kingdom of God and his righteousness before all other things? Are you hungering and thirsting after righteousness? Have you given to some one that asked of you? Tell me something that you have done, are doing, or are trying to do because he told you...

Obedience is not perfection, but trying. You count him a hard master, and will not stir. Do you suppose he ever gave a commandment knowing it was of no use for it could not be done? He tells us a thing knowing that we must do it, or be lost; that not his Father himself could save us but by getting us at length to do everything he commands, for not otherwise can we know life, can we learn the holy secret of divine being. He knows that you can try, and that in your trying and failing he will be able to help you, until at length you shall do the will of God even as he does it himself. He takes the will in the imperfect deed, and makes the deed at last perfect. Correctest notions without obedience are worthless. The doing of the will of God is the way to oneness with God, which alone is salvation. Sitting at the gate of heaven, sitting on the footstool of the throne itself, yea, clasping the knees of the Father, you could not be at peace, except in their every vital movement, in every their smallest point of consciousness, your heart, your soul, your mind, your brain, your body, were one with the living God. If you had one brooding thought that was not a joy in him, you would not be at peace; if you had one desire you could not leave absolutely to his will you would not be at peace; you would not be saved, therefore could not feel saved. God, all and in all, ours to the fulfilling of our very being, is the religion of the perfect, son-hearted Lord Christ.

George MacDonald
Unspoken Sermons

Everyone present was so astounded that people kept saying to each other, "What on earth has happened? This new teaching has authority behind it. Why, he even gives his orders to evil spirits and they obey him!" And his reputation spread like wild-fire through the whole Galilean district.

Mark 1:27,28, Phillips

"Everyone then who hears these words of mine and puts them into practice is like a sensible man who builds his house on the rock. Down came the rain and up came the floods, while the winds blew and roared upon that house—and it did not fall because its foundations were on the rock. And everyone who hears these words of mine and does not follow them can be compared with a foolish man who built his house on sand. Down came the rain and up came the floods, while the winds blew and battered that house till it collapsed, and fell with a great crash." When Jesus had finished these words the crowd were astonished at the power behind his teaching. For his words had the ring of authority, quite unlike those of the scribes.

Matthew 7:24-29, Phillips

"It is the distinctive feature of early Christian theology that it fastened upon the person of Christ as the centre of Christianity. We can conceive that a different line of thought might have been adopted. The Church might conceivably have made the moral precepts contained in the Sermon on the Mount or a belief that God is the Father of all mankind, or the experience of conversion, the dominating principle of Christianity. But while these and other great religious truths were not forgotten, they were believed to depend upon the doctrine of the person of Christ. From the very nature of the case it followed that this doctrine had an enormous influence. Every other doctrine radiated from it, and it seems to have been assumed that any one who intelligently grasped the truth about Christ would be able to anticipate or approve the rest of the teaching of the Church. Now this distinctive feature of ancient theology can be traced in the teaching of Christ himself. It is derived from an impression of a truth which was felt by the companions of Jesus. His words and His actions gradually convinced them that there was an unutterable difference between themselves and Him."

Leighton Pullan
Early Christian Doctrine

"God has always been eager to get to talking with man again. The silence is hard on Him. He is hungry to be on intimate terms again with his old friend. Of course he had to use a language that man could understand. Jesus is God spelling Himself out so man can understand. He is the A and the Z, and all between, of the Old Eden language of love."

S.D. Gordon
Quiet Talks About Jesus

"We have listened, perhaps, to other men's arguments concerning the Divinity of our Lord, conscious the while how little they were doing for us. Let us listen to Christ Himself. Let us put ourselves to school with Him, as these first disciples did, and suffer Him to make His own impression upon us. And if ours be sincere and receptive souls as were theirs, from us also He shall win the adoring cry, 'My Lord and my God.'"

George Jackson
The Teaching of Jesus

"For this is the glory of a religion of love. And this is the glory of the religion of the Lord Jesus Christ. He was anointed to comfort 'all that mourn.' The 'God of all comfort' sent His Son to be the comforter of a mourning world. And all through His life on earth He fulfilled His divine mission."

Hannah Whitall Smith
God of All Comfort

"No proofs were given of the teaching, except the truth, except the correspondence of the teaching with the truth. The whole teaching consisted in the knowledge of the truth and in following it, in a greater and ever greater approximation to it, in matters of life. According to this teaching, there are no acts which can justify a man, make him righteous; there is only the model of truth which attracts all hearts, for the inner perfection—in the person of Christ, and for the outer—in the realization of the kingdom of God. The fulfillment of the teaching is only in the motion along a given path, in the approximation to perfection—the inner—the imitation of Christ, and the outer—the establishment of the kingdom of God."

Leo Tolstoy
The Kingdom of God is Within You

I Heard the Voice of Jesus Say

1
I heard the voice of Jesus say,
"Come unto me and rest.
Lay down, O weary one,
lay down your head upon my breast."
I came to Jesus as I was,
so weary, worn, and sad.
I found in him a resting place,
and he has made me glad.

2
I heard the voice of Jesus say,
"Behold, I freely give
the living water, thirsty one;

stoop down and drink and live."
I came to Jesus, and I drank
of that life-giving stream.
My thirst was quenched, my soul revived,
and now I live in him.

3
I heard the voice of Jesus say,
"I am the dawning light.
Look unto me, your morn shall rise,
and all your day be bright."
I looked to Jesus, and I found
in him my star, my sun,
and in that light of life I'll walk
till trav'ling days are done.

Horatius Bonar

A Prayer

Jesus, open my heart to the wonder of your words. Today, teach me to feast on your teachings and parables and simple thoughts. May I find rest by simply reading, listening, pondering and obeying what you've said. Tell me what to do—and I'll do it.

What is your word for *this* day, Lord Jesus?

In your name.

Amen.

The Cross of Jesus

All, Without Exception

John Calvin
1553

And the people stood gazing, and the rulers along with them mocked him, saying, "He saved others, let him save himself, if he is the Christ, the elect of God." The soldiers also mocked him, approaching, and offering him vinegar, And saying, "If thou art the King of the Jews, save thyself." ... And one of the malefactors, who were executed, reviled him, saying, "If thou art the Christ, save thyself and us." And the other answering, rebuked him, saying, "Dost not thou at least fear God, since thou art in the same condemnation? And we indeed justly; for we receive what is due to our actions, but this man hath done nothing amiss." And he said to Jesus, "Lord, remember me, when thou shalt come into thy kingdom." Jesus said to him, "Verily, I say to thee, Today shalt thou be with me in paradise."

—Luke 23:35-43

"LORD, REMEMBER ME." I know not that, since the creation of the world, there ever was a more remarkable and striking example of faith; and so much the greater admiration is due to the grace of the Holy Spirit, of which it affords so magnificent a display.

A robber, who not only had not been educated in the school of Christ, but, by giving himself up to execrable murders, had endeavored to extinguish all sense of what was right, suddenly rises higher than all the apostles and the other disciples whom the Lord himself had taken so much pains to instruct; and not only so, but he adores Christ as a *King* while on the gallows, celebrates his *kingdom* in the midst of shocking and worse than revolting abasement, and declares him, when dying, to be the Author of life. Even though he had formerly possessed right faith, and heard many things about the office of Christ, and had even been confirmed in it by his miracles, still that knowledge might have been overpowered by the thick darkness of so disgraceful a death. But that a person, ignorant and uneducated, and whose mind was altogether corrupted, should all at once, on receiving his earliest instructions, perceive salvation and heavenly glory in the accursed cross, was truly astonishing. For what marks or ornaments of royalty did he see in Christ, so as to raise his mind to his kingdom? And, certainly, this was, as it were, from the depth of hell to rise above the heavens. To the flesh it must have appeared to be fabulous and absurd, to ascribe to one who was *rejected and despised*, (Isaiah 53:3) whom the world could not endure, an earthly kingdom more exalted than all the empires of the world. Hence we infer how acute must have been the eyes of his mind, by which he beheld life in death, exaltation in ruin, glory in shame, victory in destruction, a *kingdom* in bondage...

"Verily I tell thee." Though Christ had not yet made a public triumph over death, still he displays the efficacy and fruit of his death in the midst of his humiliation. And in this way he shows that he never was deprived of the power of his kingdom; for nothing more lofty or magnificent belongs to a divine King, than to restore life to the dead. So then, Christ, although, struck by the hand of God, he appeared to be a man utterly abandoned, yet as he did not cease to be the Savior of the world, he was always endued with heavenly power for fulfilling his office. And, first, we ought to observe his inconceivable readiness in so kindly receiving the robber without delay, and promising to make him a partaker of a happy life. There is therefore no room to doubt that he is prepared to admit into his kingdom all, without exception, who shall apply to him. Hence we may conclude with certainty that we shall be saved, provided that he *remember us*; and it is impossible that he shall forget those who commit to him their salvation.

But if a robber found the entrance into heaven so easy, because, while he beheld on all sides ground for total despair, he relied on the grace of Christ; much more will Christ, who has now vanquished death, stretch out his hand to us from his throne, to admit us to be partakers of life. For since Christ has *nailed to his cross the handwriting which was opposed to us* (Col. 2:14) and has destroyed death and Satan, and in his resurrection has triumphed over *the prince of the world*, (John 12:31) it would be unreasonable to suppose that the passage from death to life will be more laborious and difficult to us than to the robber. Whoever then in dying shall commit to Christ, in true faith, the keeping of his soul, will not be long detained or allowed to languish in suspense; but Christ will meet his prayer with the same kindness which he exercised towards *the robber*. Away, then, with that detestable contrivance of the Sophists about retaining the punishment when the guilt is removed; for we see how Christ, in acquitting him from condemnation, frees him also from punishment. Nor is this inconsistent with the fact, that the robber nevertheless endures to the very last the punishment which had been pronounced upon him; for we must not here imagine any compensation which serves the purpose of satisfaction for appeasing the judgment of God, (as the Sophists dream,) but the Lord merely trains his elect by corporal punishments to displeasure and hatred of sin. Thus, when the robber has been brought by fatherly discipline to self-denial Christ receives him, as it were, into his bosom, and does not send him away to the fire...

We ought likewise to observe by what keys the gate of heaven was opened to the robber;... Christ is satisfied with repentance and faith, so as to receive him willingly when he comes to him. And this confirms more fully what I formerly suggested, that if any man disdain to abide by the footsteps of the robber, and to follow in his path, he deserves everlasting destruction, because by wicked pride he shuts against himself the gate of heaven. And, certainly, as Christ has given to all of us, in the person of *the robber*, a general pledge of obtaining forgiveness, so, on the other hand, he has bestowed on this wretched man such distinguished honor, in order that, laying aside our own glory, we may glory in nothing but the mercy of God alone. If each of us shall truly and seriously examine the subject, we shall find abundant reason to be ashamed of the prodigious mass of our crimes, so that we shall not be offended at having for our guide and leader a poor wretch, who obtained salvation by free grace. Again, as the death of Christ at that time yielded its fruit, so we infer from it that souls, when they have departed from their bodies, continue to live; otherwise the promise of Christ, which he confirms even by an oath, would be a mockery.

"Today shalt thou be with me in paradise." We ought not to enter into curious and subtle arguments about the place of paradise. Let us rest satisfied with knowing that those who are engrafted by faith into the body of Christ are partakers of that life, and thus enjoy after death a

blessed and joyful rest, until the perfect glory of the heavenly life is fully manifested by the coming of Christ....

John Calvin
Commentary on Matthew, Mark & Luke

> *You, who were spiritually dead because of your sins and your uncircumcision,[2] God has now made to share in the very life of Christ! He has forgiven you all your sins: Christ has utterly wiped out the damning evidence of broken laws and commandments which always hung over our heads, and has completely annulled it by nailing it over his own head on the cross. And then having drawn the sting of all the powers ranged against us, he exposed them, shattered, empty and defeated, in his final glorious triumphant act!*

Colossians 2:13-15, Phillips

"What, then, was Jesus doing in his life and in his death? The answer must be that in his life and in his death Jesus was demonstrating to men the eternal, unchangeable, unconquerable love of God. He was demonstrating to men that God is the Father who loves undefeatably and whose one desire is that the lost son should come home. When Jesus entered the world, when he healed the sick, comforted the sad, fed the hungry, forgave his enemies, he was saying to men: 'God loves you like that.' When he died upon the cross, he was saying: 'Nothing that men can ever do to God will stop God loving them. There is no limit to the love of God. There is no end beyond which that love will not go. God loves you like that.' That is why nothing less than death on the Cross would do. If Jesus had refused or escaped the Cross, if he had not died, it would have meant that there was some point in suffering and sorrow at which the love of God stopped, that there was some point beyond which forgiveness was impossible. But the Cross is God saying in Jesus: 'There is no limit to which my love will not go and no sin which my love cannot forgive.'

---

2   i.e. the fact that you were outside the Law

"The work of Christ is not something *about which* a man must know; it is something which he must experience in his own heart and mind and life. It is not so much to be understood as it is to be appropriated. For that reason it is not enough to know how others have interpreted it. It is quite true that it would be arrogant and presumptuous folly completely to disregard the great classical interpretations of it; but nevertheless each man must interpret it for himself. But it can only be interpreted from the inside. In the preface to his *Cur Deus Homo*, Anselm said: 'Some men seek for reasons because they do not believe; we seek for them because we do believe.' Any consideration of the work of Christ must be not so much argument as witness. How then are we to interpret it for ourselves?

"One thing I know—that because of Jesus Christ and because of what he is and did and does my whole relationship to God is changed. Because of Jesus Christ I know that God is my father and friend. Daily and hourly I experience the fact that I can enter into his presence with confidence and boldness. He is no longer my enemy; he is no longer even my judge; there is no longer any unbridgeable gulf between him and me; I am more at home with God than I am with any human being in the human world. And all this is so because of Jesus Christ, and it could not possibly have happened without him."

William Barclay
The Mind of Jesus

"Out of all His words and works and limbs and nerves, He made a cord, and drew us so skillfully, and so heartily, that the bloody sweat poured from His sacred Body. And when He had drawn men without ceasing for three and thirty years, He saw the beginnings of a movement and the redemption of all things that would follow. Therefore He said, 'And I, if I be lifted up on the Cross, will draw all men unto Me.'"

Meister Eckhart
from the sermon "The Attractive Power of God"

"Jesus Christ loved all men, He tasted death for all men, He intercedes for all men. Let us ask then, are we the imitators, the representatives, and the executors of Jesus Christ? Then must we in our prayers run parallel with His atonement in its extent. The atoning blood of Jesus Christ gives sanctity and efficiency to our prayers. As worldwide, as broad, and as human as the man Christ Jesus was, so must be our prayers. The intercessions of Christ's people must give currency and expedition to the work of Christ, carry the atoning blood to its benignant ends, and help to strike off the chains of sin from every ransomed soul. We must be as praying, as tearful, and as compassionate as was Christ."

E.M. Bounds
The Reality of Prayer

"His was a death of *peace*, nay, of *triumph*! Ere He closed His eyes, light broke through the curtains of thick darkness. In the calm composure of filial confidence He breathed away His soul—'Father, into Thy hands I commend My spirit!' What was the secret of such tranquillity? This is His own key to it—'I have glorified Thee on the earth; I have finished the work which Thou gavest me to do.'"

John R. MacDuff
The Mind of Jesus

"[This] was the answer of God to the world which nailed Christ to the cross: blessing. God does not repay like with like, and neither should the righteous person. No condemning, no railing, but blessing. The world would have not hope if this were not so. The world lives and has its future by means of the blessing of God and of the righteous person. Blessing means laying one's hands upon something and saying: You belong to God in spite of all. It is in this way that we respond to the world which causes us such suffering. We do not forsake it, cast it out, despise or condemn it. Instead, we recall it to God, we give it hope, we lay our hands upon it and say: God's blessing come upon you; may God renew you; be blessed, you dear God-created world, for you belong to your creator and redeemer."

Dietrich Bonhoeffer
Meditating on the Word

"No one who follows the Crucified is called only to life's delights, nor would he wish to be. When we taste the myrrh, do not let us forget the loving words, 'Drink, yea, drink abundantly, O beloved.' Let us not drink unwillingly, but with a generous trust in the love that says, *I* have drunk of that cup; drink, O beloved."

Amy Carmichael
Edges of His Ways

And Can It Be That I Should Gain

1
And can it be that I should gain
An int'rest in the Savior's blood?
Died He for me, who caused His pain?
For me, who Him to death pursued?
Amazing love! how can it be
That Thou, my God, should die for me?

Refrain:
Amazing love! how can it be
That Thou, my God, should die for me!

2
'Tis mystery all! Th'Immortal dies!
Who can explore His strange design?
In vain the firstborn seraph tries
To sound the depths of love divine!
'Tis mercy all! let earth adore,
Let angel minds inquire no more. [Refrain]

3
He left His Father's throne above,
So free, so infinite His grace;
Emptied Himself of all but love,
And bled for Adam's helpless race;
'Tis mercy all, immense and free;
For, O my God, it found out me. [Refrain]

4
Long my imprisoned spirit lay
Fast bound in sin and nature's night;
Thine eye diffused a quick'ning ray,
I woke, the dungeon flamed with light;
My chains fell off, my heart was free;
I rose, went forth and followed Thee. [Refrain]

5
No condemnation now I dread;
Jesus, and all in Him is mine!
Alive in Him, my living Head,
And clothed in righteousness divine,
Bold I approach th'eternal throne,
And claim the crown, through Christ my own. [Refrain]

Amen.

Charles Wesley

A Prayer

Jesus, I struggle to believe that I am really and truly free from sin. I "believe" in your Cross, but sometimes I forget what it means. Please teach me afresh what it truly means.

I want to believe that you have already set me free from everything I've ever done wrong and that you've exchanged my nature for a new nature like yours. I want to learn how powerful is your death for me.

Teach me how to live today as the freest person I've ever met: a person totally free and faultless in your sight.

O Jesus, I want to be free in you!

In your name.

Amen.

The Resurrection of Jesus

Unspeakably Rich and Happy Now

Alfred Eldersheim
1883

IT WAS THE EARLY AFTERNOON of that spring-day, perhaps soon after the early meal, when two men from that circle of disciples left the City. Their narrative affords deeply interesting glimpses into the circle of the Church in those first days. The impression conveyed to us is of utter bewilderment, in which only some things stood out unshaken and firm: love to the Person of Jesus; love among the brethren; mutual confidence and fellowship; together with a dim hope of something yet to come—if not Christ in His Kingdom, yet some manifestation of, or approach to it. The Apostolic College seems broken up into units; even the two chief Apostles, Peter and John, are only 'certain of them that were with us.' And no wonder; for they are no longer 'Apostles'—sent out. Who is to send them forth? Not a dead Christ! And what would be their commission, and to whom and whither? And above all rested a cloud of utter uncertainty and perplexity. Jesus *was* a Prophet mighty in word and deed before God and all the people. But their rulers had crucified Him. What was to be their new relation to Jesus; what to their rulers? And what of the great hope of the Kingdom, which they had connected with Him?

Thus they were unclear on that very Easter Day even as to His Mission and Work: unclear as to the past, the present, and the future. What need for the Resurrection, and for the teaching which the Risen One alone could bring! These two men had on that very day been in communication with Peter and John. And it leaves on us the impression that, amidst the general confusion, all had brought such tidings as they, or had come to hear them, and had tried but failed, to put it all into order or to see light around it. 'The women' had come to tell of the empty Tomb and of their vision of Angels, who said that He was alive. But as yet the Apostles had no explanation to offer. Peter and John had gone to see for themselves. They had brought back confirmation of the report that the Tomb was empty, but they had seen neither Angels nor

Him Whom they were said to have declared alive. And, although the two had evidently left the circle of the disciples, if not Jerusalem, before the Magdalene came, yet we know that even her account did not carry conviction to the minds of those that heard it.

Of the two, who on that early spring afternoon left the City in company, we know that one bore the name of Cleopas. The other, unnamed, has for that very reason, and because the narrative of that work bears in its vividness the character of personal recollection, been identified with St. Luke himself. If so, then, as has been finely remarked, each of the Gospels would, like a picture, bear in some dim corner the indication of its author: the first, that of the 'publican;' that by St. Mark, that of the young man, who, in the night of the Betrayal, had fled from his captors; that of St. Luke in the Companion of Cleopas; and that of St. John, in the disciple whom Jesus loved. Uncertainty, almost equal to that about the second traveller to Emmaus, rests on the identification of that place. But such great probability attaches, if not to the exact spot, yet to the locality, or rather the valley, that we may in imagination follow the two companies on their road.

We leave the City by the Western Gate. A rapid progress for about twenty-five minutes, and we have reached the edge of the plateau. The blood-stained City, and the cloud-and-gloom-capped trying-place of the followers of Jesus, are behind us; and with every step forward and upward the air seems fresher and freer, as if we felt in it the scent of mountains, or even the far-off breezes of the sea. Another twenty-five or thirty minutes—perhaps a little more, passing here and there country-houses—and we pause to look back, now on the wide prospect far as Bethlehem. Again we pursue our way. We are now getting beyond the dreary, rocky region, and are entering on a valley. To our right is the pleasant spot that marks the ancient *Nephtoah*, on the border of Judah, now occupied by the village of *Lifta*. A short quarter of an hour more, and we have left the well-paved Roman road and are heading up a lovely valley. The path gently climbs in a north-westerly direction, with the height on which Emmaus stands prominently before us. About equidistant are, on the right Lifta, on the left Kolonieh. The roads from these two, describing almost a semicircle (the one to the north-west, the other to the north-east), meet about a quarter of a mile to the south of Emmaus (Hammoza, Beit Mizza). What an oasis this in a region of hills! Along the course of the stream, which babbles down, and low in the valley crossed by a bridge, are scented orange-and lemon-gardens, olive-groves, luscious fruit trees, pleasant enclosures, shady nooks, bright dwellings, and on the height lovely Emmaus. A sweet spot to which to wander on that spring afternoon; a most suitable place where to meet such companionship, and to find such teaching, as on that Easter Day.

It may have been where the two roads from Lifta and Kolonieh meet, that the mysterious Stranger, Whom they knew not, their eyes being 'holden,' joined the two friends. Yet all these six or seven miles their converse had been of Him, and even now their flushed faces bore the marks of sadness on account of those events of which they had been speaking—disappointed hopes, all the more bitter for the perplexing tidings about the empty Tomb and the absent Body of the Christ. So is Christ often near to us when our eyes are holden, and we know Him not; and so do ignorance and unbelief often fill our hearts with sadness, even when truest joy would most become us. To the question of the Stranger about the topics of a conversation which had so visibly affected them, they replied in language which shows that they were so absorbed by it themselves, as scarcely to understand how even a festive pilgrim and stranger in Jerusalem could have failed to know it, or perceive its supreme importance. Yet, strangely unsympathetic as from His question He might seem, there was that in His Appearance which unlocked their inmost hearts. They told Him their thoughts about this Jesus; how He had showed Himself a prophet mighty in deed and word before God and all the people; then, how their rulers had crucified Him; and, lastly, how fresh perplexity had come to them from the tidings which the women had brought, and which Peter and John had so far confirmed, but were unable to explain. Their words were almost childlike in their simplicity, deeply truthful, and with a pathos and earnest craving for guidance and comfort that goes straight to the heart. To such souls it was that the Risen Saviour would give His first teaching. The very rebuke with which He opened it must have brought its comfort. We also, in our weakness, are sometimes sore distrest when we hear what, at the moment, seem to us insuperable difficulties raised to any of the great of our holy faith; and, in perhaps equal weakness, feel comforted and strengthened, when some 'great one' turns them aside, or avows himself in face of them a believing disciple of Christ. As if man's puny height could reach up to heaven's mysteries, or any big infant's strength were needed to steady the building which God has reared on that great Cornerstone! But Christ's rebuke was not of such kind. Their sorrow arose from their folly in looking only at the things seen, and this, from their slowness to believe what the prophets had spoken. Had they attended to this, instead of allowing it all? Did not the Scriptures with one voice teach this twofold truth about the Messiah, that He was to suffer and to enter into His glory? Then why wonder—why not rather expect, that He had suffered, and that Angels had proclaimed Him alive again?

He spake it, and fresh hope sprang up in their hearts, new thoughts rose in their minds. Their eager gaze was fastened on Him as He now opened up, one by one, the Scriptures, from Moses and all the prophets, and in each well-remembered passage interpreted to them the things concerning Himself. Oh, that we had been there to hear—though in silence of our hearts also, if only we crave for it, and if we walk with Him, He sometimes so opens from the Scriptures—nay, from all the Scriptures, that which comes not to us by critical study: 'the things concerning Himself.' All too quickly fled the moments. The brief space was traversed, and the Stranger seemed about to pass on from Emmaus—not feigning it, but really: for the Christ will only abide with us if our longing and loving constrain Him. But they could not part with Him. 'They constrained Him.' Love made them ingenious. It was toward evening; the day was far spent; He must even abide with them. What rush of thought and feeling comes to us, as we think of it all, and try to realise time, scenes, circumstances in our experience, that are blessedly akin to it.

The Master allowed Himself to be constrained. He went in to be their guest, as they thought, for the night. The simple evening-meal was spread. He sat down with them to the frugal board. And now He was no longer the Stranger; He was the Master. No one asked, or questioned, as He took the bread and spake the words of blessing, then, breaking, gave it to them. But that moment it was, as if an unfelt Hand had been taken from their eyelids, as if suddenly the film had been cleared from their sight. And as they knew Him, He vanished from their view—for that which He had come to do had been done. They were unspeakably rich and happy now. But, amidst it all, one thing forced itself ever anew upon them, that, even while their eyes had yet been holden, their hearts had burned within them, while He spake to them and opened to them the Scriptures. So, then, they had learned to full the Resurrection-lesson—not only that He was risen indeed, but that it needed not His seen Bodily Presence, if only He opened up to the heart and mind all the Scriptures concerning Himself. And this, concerning those other words about 'holding' and 'touching' Him—about having converse and fellowship with Him as the Risen One, had been also the lesson taught the Magdalene, when He would not suffer her loving, worshipful touch, pointing her to the Ascension before Him. This is the great lesson concerning the Risen One, which the Church fully learned in the Day of Pentecost.

Alfred Eldersheim
The Life and Times of Jesus the Messiah

> *For he has rescued us from all that is really evil and called us to a life of holiness—not because of any of our achievements but for his own purpose. Before time began he planned to give us in Christ the grace to achieve this purpose, but it is only since our saviour Jesus Christ has been revealed that the method has become apparent. For Christ has completely abolished death, and has now, through the Gospel, opened to us men the shining possibilities of the life that is eternal. It is this Gospel that I am commissioned to proclaim; it is of this Gospel that I am appointed both messenger and teacher, and it is for this Gospel that I am now suffering these things. Yet I am not in the least ashamed. For I know the one in whom I have placed my confidence, and I am perfectly certain that the work he has committed to me is safe in his hands until that day.*
>
> **2 Timothy 1:9-12, Phillips**

"Christ recovered for the human race not merely what Adam had lost through sin, but all that Adam could have attained through merit. For Christ's power to merit was far greater than that of man prior to sin.

By sin Adam incurred the necessity of dying because he lost the power which would have enabled him to avoid death if he had not sinned. Christ not only did away with the necessity of dying, but even gained the power of not being able to die."

Thomas Aquinas
The Compendium of Theology

"Little by little as He spoke, His Disciples' faces lighted up with a forgotten hope, and their eyes shone with exaltation. This was the hour of consolation after the gloom of those dreadful days just passed. His indubitable presence showed that the impossible was assured, that God had not abandoned them and never would abandon them. Their enemies, apparently victorious, were conquered; the visible truth bore out all the prophecies. It was true that they had known already everything He was then saying, but those truths really lived in them only when His lips repeated them... Their King had come back, the Kingdom was near at hand, and His brothers, instead of being derided and persecuted, would reign with Him through all eternity."

Giovanni Papini
Life of Christ

"What made those babblers so eloquent; those ignorant and illiterate men so profoundly skilled in the mysteries of redemption; those cowards so courageous, as to despise every danger, and maintain the truth amidst the most terrible sufferings? This change could not have been effected by their Master, if he was still lying in the grave; and it is, therefore, a proof that he had risen from it, and performed the promise which we shall immediately proceed to consider."

John Dick
Lectures on the Acts of the Apostles

"We need firmly to hold on to the fact that there is no death for the Christian; it has been completely abolished. For the old dark god[3] with his weapons of basic, primitive fear still operates, quite illegitimately, in many Christian hearts. We should allow him no foothold, for he has no right to be there, and he has no real power over us. The glory of Easter is not a pious hope that we shall somehow survive after a fear-ridden journey through the 'gloomy portal.' It is a demonstration of undiluted joy. Christ is the one who bore the sin, the darkness, the terror, and the pain. He is the one who 'tasted death for every man'...

"It was this unforgettable demonstration of power, power released into those dark areas of human being where no man had ever triumphed before, that gave the young Church not only its unshakeable conviction, but also its...unconquerable courage. For to them, as surely it should be to us, the resurrection was no mere happy ending to an otherwise ghastly tragedy. It was a demonstration of power, shown once historically in time, on one unique occasion. It was also the birth of a new power altogether, a new weapon and a new resource for the liberation and life of men."

J.B. Phillips
Good News

"Our gospel is the most pessimistic of faiths in that it dared to look at life through a cross, but it is the most optimistic of faiths in that it now looks at life through an Easter morning. It puts an unconquerable courage at the heart of life, so that whenever the real gospel is accepted, there life lifts up its head, there it refuses to be beaten; it finds its moral courage to live."

E. Stanley Jones
The Christ of Every Road

---

[3] i.e. Death

"On the third day the friends of Christ coming at daybreak to the place found the grave empty and the stone rolled away. In varying ways they realised the new wonder; but even they hardly realised that the world had died in the night. What they were looking at was the first day of a new creation, with a new heaven and a new earth; and in a semblance of the gardener God walked again in the garden, in the cool not of the evening but the dawn."

G.K. Chesterton
The Everlasting Man

"In Christ we have an ever-growing revelation. He is the resurrection and the life. As we know him we know our future."

George MacDonald
The Miracles of Our Lord

No Coward Soul Is Mine

No coward soul is mine
No trembler in the world's storm-troubled sphere
I see Heaven's glories shine
And Faith shines equal arming me from Fear

O God within my breast
Almighty ever-present Deity
Life, that in me hast rest,
As I Undying Life, have power in Thee

Vain are the thousand creeds
That move men's hearts, unutterably vain,
Worthless as withered weeds
Or idlest froth amid the boundless main

To waken doubt in one
Holding so fast by thy infinity,

So surely anchored on
The steadfast rock of Immortality.

With wide-embracing love
Thy spirit animates eternal years
Pervades and broods above,
Changes, sustains, dissolves, creates and rears

Though earth and moon were gone
And suns and universes ceased to be
And Thou wert left alone
Every Existence would exist in thee

There is not room for Death
Nor atom that his might could render void
Since thou art Being and Breath
And what thou art may never be destroyed.

Emily Brontë

A Prayer

Jesus, you are alive! I'm talking to *you* right now! Just as surely as I would talk to a living, breathing human being standing right next to me, I may talk to you at any time!

Jesus, you are—*alive!*

Help me to live today fearlessly, totally unafraid of life and death, because of the way you lived and died and lived again! Teach me how you want me to live, O Risen Jesus!

I am enamored with you!

You are alive—*and I am yours!*

In your name, Jesus.

Amen.

The Resurrection of Jesus

The Ascension of Jesus

Divinity Blazing Forth

Augustine of Hippo
5th Century, A.D.

WHY ISN'T ASCENSION DAY a day of feasting and fellowship like Christmas? Christmas gave Jesus Christ our Savior to earth; the Ascension restored him to heaven. At Christmas he deigned to assume our humanity; on the day of his Ascension he manifested his divinity. Christmas bespeaks the grace which springs inexhaustibly from his humility; the Ascension confirms our faith in his adorable Godhead. Christmas presents him coming forth from a virginal womb; the Ascension shows him going to occupy the very throne of God. On Christmas day he comes down to redeem us; at the Ascension he goes up to intercede for us. At Christmas his Father sends him; at the Ascension his Father receives him. (We know, however, that he was never separated from his Father—even when dwelling among us. Though visiting earth, he didn't leave heaven.)

How great a solemnity this day is, my brothers and sisters, when Jesus our Redeemer so powerfully proclaims his divinity, and is seen rising to heaven solely to show us all the more clearly that he descended to earth. "No one," he states, "has gone up to heaven except him who has come down from heaven—the Son of Man." (Jn. 3:13) And a psalmist had long before sung: "He came from highest heaven, and he returns to highest heaven." (Ps. 19:6) Having concealed himself from everyone's gaze on coming down to earth, he wants his Ascension to be all the more visible. At his Incarnation, nothing had impressed the human eye; but at his Ascension, everything had to be manifest and plain to see, in order to strengthen our faith.

The Lord is full of mercy and pity. So when he comes solely to redeem and save us, we see his humanity alone as he embraces opprobrium, torture, crucifixion, burial and all the outward symptoms of human infirmity, thus becoming an object of scandal for haughty unbelievers. But if on Christmas day he chose only abasement and humiliation in order to save us, on the day of his Ascension he willed to have the full splendor of his divinity blaze forth, so that we, having deemed him a man among men, might proclaim him to be truly God.

Scripture informs us that, after his passion, our God and Savior presented himself alive to the Apostles, gave them abundant proof of his Resurrection, and spoke to them about the kingdom of God for forty days. (Acts 1:3) After enduring the cross and death, and before rising to heaven, Jesus also appeared to many persons on earth during these forty days which—from Easter till today—we spend in holy freedom because they're a time, not of sadness, but of joy, in keeping with our Savior's words: "Can the wedding guests mourn while the bridegroom is with them?" (Mt 9:15)

Once those days were over, and "as all the disciples were looking on, he was lifted up, and a cloud took him from their sight." (Acts 1:9) Let the Jews listen to that statement; let the Gentiles listen and be astounded. They jeered at him as he hung upon the cross. So let them now ponder the account of his Ascension into heaven. They cited the humiliations of Calvary. So let them now bear witness to the splendors of this day.

Next we read: "Suddenly two men dressed in white stood beside them and said, 'Men of Galilee, why are you standing there looking at the sky? This Jesus who has been taken from you into heaven will return in the same way you have seen him going into heaven.'" (Acts 1:11) So, after accomplishing his mission on earth, Jesus had just returned to heaven when celestial envoys came to confirm what the disciples had seen, and to reassure them that they weren't the victims of some illusion, thus enabling them to attest personally not only to the fact of the Savior's Ascension but also to his promised return to earth at the end of the world.

The Gospels contain the same teaching as the book of Acts: "He led them as far as Bethany and raised his hands in blessing. As he blessed the disciples, he parted from them and was taken up to heaven. They paid him homage and then returned to Jerusalem with great joy." (Lk. 24:51–52)

Because the Savior abased himself for us, it is for us also that he displays a wholly divine splendor in his person. From the celestial throne which is his by right, he shows us that heaven is now open to us. Not content with having saved mankind, he wants to glorify it. And so our humanity, in which he deigned to clothe himself, today makes its triumphal entry into heaven. What an honor for the clay of which we are made, since it now reigns in heaven!

Having fasted for forty days in preparation for Easter, we rejoiced for another forty days after. The first forty ended with the feast of the Resurrection, and the second forty end with today's great solemnity of the Ascension, on which our Savior deprives us of his visible presence— without, however, ceasing to dwell with us. While he was physically in our midst, he was not separated from his Father; likewise, now that he has returned to his Father, he's not separated from us. Far from deserting us like strangers, he remains with us and lives in our midst, as he personally reassures us: "Do not let your hearts be troubled or afraid… I am going away, but I will come back to you." (Jn. 14:1, 27–28)

Therefore, Jesus is living among us, consoling those who suffer anguish and pain, helping those in danger, assisting the unfortunate and the afflicted. I repeat: Jesus is with us, present not only in our labors but also in our words and our thoughts. Scrutinizing and fathoming our very heart, he sees what our senses, our hands and our minds beget. How well ordered, then, our life should be; how pious and chaste, since we're always under God's watchful eyes!

You're well aware of this doctrine, my brothers and sisters. Neglectful servants cringe and fawn when their earthly master is present, and they don't cut themselves any slack unless they're sure he's not watching. You Christians, however, know full well that you can never hide from the Lord's gaze.

Wherever you go, you carry your conscience with you. If those lax servants I mentioned before were in their master's presence day and night, do you think they'd ever allow themselves to disobey his orders? Since God is present everywhere and, therefore, is always with you, what docility should awe and respect for his presence inspire in you! In his mercy, he'll always be here to protect us; but he'll also be here as the witness and avenger of all our failings.

To this God, who is as good as he is just, and as terrible as he is merciful, be honor and glory for ever and ever. Amen.

Augustine of Hippo
"On the Ascension of Our Lord"

God, who gave our forefathers many different glimpses of the truth in the words of the prophets, has now, at the end of the present age, given us the truth in the Son. Through the Son God made the whole universe, and to the Son he has ordained that all creation shall ultimately belong. This Son, radiance of the glory of God, flawless expression of the nature of God, himself the upholding principle of all that is, effected in person the reconciliation between God and man and then took his seat at the right hand of the majesty on high....

Hebrews 1:1-3, Phillips

"Christ's ascension was the exaltation of man to the right hand of God. It was as Man He entered heaven and sat upon His throne. It is as the Son of Man, with a human face and form, that He is sitting there today. It is in our behalf that He has gone up to God. He claims our place there, and keeps it till we come. What an honor to the once lost human race was the ascension of Christ! It was the entrance of a Man to the highest place in the heavenly world, with the first-fruits of this new race following in His train and taking a place with Him that angels could not claim. Lord, what is man that Thou hast set Thine heart upon him and so strangely redeemed and lifted him up for ever? Oh, let us rejoice and shout for joy as we see the Son of God ascend and write our names upon the seats of glory, as our Great Forerunner! God has recognized man's right to enter heaven, to enter it as a King, to enter its highest place of dignity and blessing through the ascension of the Son of Man."

A.B. Simpson
The Christ of the Forty Days

"The Lord, in the glory of His risen life, and in the riches of the gifts which He received when He ascended up on high, is the pattern for us, and the power which fulfils its own pattern. In Him we see what man may become, and what His followers must become. The limits of that power will not be reached until every Christian soul is perfectly assimilated to that likeness, and bears all its beauty in its face, nor till every Christian soul is raised to participation in Christ's dignity and sits on His throne."

Alexander Maclaren
Expositions of Holy Scripture

Thy face is now my fatherland,—
The radiant sunshine of my days,—
My realm of love, my sunlit land,
Where, all life long, I sing Thy praise;
It is the lily of the vale,
Whose mystic perfume, freely given,
Brings comfort, when I faint and fail,
And makes me taste the peace of heaven.

Thérèse of Lisieux

"We who feel ourselves alienated from the fellowship of God can now raise our discouraged heads and look up. Through the virtues of Christ's atoning death the cause of our banishment has been removed. We may return as the Prodigal returned, and be welcome. As we approach the Garden, our home before the Fall, the flaming sword is withdrawn. The keepers of the tree of life stand aside when they see a son of grace approaching."

A.W. Tozer
The Knowledge of the Holy

"Look up and see the great God upon His throne. He is Love—an unceasing and inexpressible desire to communicate His own goodness and blessedness to all His creatures. He longs and delights to bless. He has inconceivably glorious purposes concerning every one of His children, by the power of His Holy Spirit, to reveal in them His love and power. He waits with all the longings of a father's heart."

Andrew Murray
Waiting on God

"Christ is already in that place of peace, which is all in all. He is on the right hand of God. He is hidden in the brightness of the radiance which issues from the everlasting throne. He is in the very abyss of peace, where there is no voice of tumult or distress, but a deep stillness—stillness, that greatest and most awful of all goods which we can fancy; that most perfect of joys, the utter profound, ineffable tranquillity of the Divine Essence. He has entered into His rest. That is our home; here we are on a pilgrimage, and Christ calls us to His many mansions which He has prepared."

John Henry Newman
from a sermon

The Hold-fast

I threaten'd to observe the strict decree
Of my dear God with all my power and might;
But I was told by one it could not be;
Yet I might trust in God to be my light.
"Then will I trust," said I, "in Him alone."
"Nay, e'en to trust in Him was also His:
We must confess that nothing is our own."
"Then I confess that He my succour is."
"But to have nought is ours, not to confess
That we have nought." I stood amaz'd at this,
Much troubled, till I heard a friend express
That all things were more ours by being His;
What Adam had, and forfeited for all,
Christ keepeth now, who cannot fail or fall.

George Herbert

A Prayer

Jesus, thank you that you lived for me, died for me, rose for me, and that you have returned to Heaven to make a way for me there. Thank you that you are with me now, that I am with you now, that we will never be apart—forever and ever.

Truly teach me what it means that, as a human being, you are presently ruling and reigning in the Throne Room of Heaven. Please make my life to be "on earth as it is in Heaven." Please rule and reign—within my life.

I long to know you more.

I long to trust you more.

I long to love you more.

In your name, Jesus.

Amen.

Learning to Approach the Throne of Grace with Confidence

Abiding in the Glorified One

Andrew Murray
1864

"Your life is hid with Christ in God. When Christ, who is our life, shall appear, then shall ye also appear with him in glory."
—Colossians 3:3-4

HE THAT ABIDES in Christ the Crucified One, learns to know what it is to be crucified with Him, and in Him to be indeed dead unto sin. He that abides in Christ the Risen and Glorified One, becomes in the same way partaker of His resurrection life, and of the glory with which He has now been crowned in heaven. Unspeakable are the blessings which flow to the soul from the union with Jesus in His glorified life.

This life is a life of *perfect victory and rest*. Before His death, the Son of God had to suffer and to struggle, could be tempted and troubled by sin and its assaults: as the Risen One, He has triumphed over sin; and, as the Glorified One, His humanity has entered into participation of the glory of Deity. The believer who abides in Him as such, is led to see how the power of sin and the flesh are indeed destroyed: the consciousness of complete and everlasting deliverance becomes increasingly clear, and the blessed rest and peace, the fruit of such a conviction that victory and deliverance are an accomplished fact, take possession of the life. Abiding in Jesus, in whom he has been raised and set in the heavenly places, he receives of that glorious life streaming from the Head through every member of the body.

This life is a life in *the full fellowship of the Father's love and holiness*. Jesus often gave prominence to this thought with His disciples. His death was a going to the Father. He prayed: "Glorify me, O Father, *with Thyself*, with the glory which I had *with Thee*." As the believer, abiding in Christ the Glorified One, seeks to realize and experience what His union with Jesus on the throne implies, he apprehends how the unclouded light of the Father's presence is His highest glory and blessedness, and in

Him the believer's portion too. He learns the sacred art of always, in fellowship with His exalted Head, dwelling in the secret of the Father's presence. Further, when Jesus was on earth, temptation could still reach Him: in glory, everything is holy, and in perfect harmony with the will of God. And so the believer who abides in Him experiences that in this high fellowship his spirit is sanctified into growing harmony with the Father's will. The heavenly life of Jesus is the power that casts out sin.

This life is a life of *loving beneficence and activity*. Seated on His throne, He dispenses His gifts, bestows His Spirit, and never ceases in love to watch and to work for those who are His. The believer cannot abide in Jesus the Glorified One, without feeling himself stirred and strengthened to work: the Spirit and the love of Jesus breathe the will and the power to be a blessing to others. Jesus went to heaven with the very object of obtaining power there to bless abundantly. He does this as the heavenly Vine only through the medium of His people as His branches. Whoever, therefore, abides in Him, the Glorified One, bears much fruit, for he receives of the Spirit and the power of the eternal life of his exalted Lord, and becomes the channel through which the fulness of Jesus, who hath been exalted to be a Prince and a Saviour, flows out to bless those around him.

There is one more thought in regard to this life of the Glorified One, and ours in Him. It is a life of *wondrous expectation and hope*. It is so with Christ. He sits at the right hand of God, *expecting* till all His enemies be made His footstool, looking forward to the time when He shall receive His full reward, when His glory shall be made manifest, and His beloved people be ever with Him in that glory. The hope of Christ is the hope of His redeemed: "I will come again and take you to myself, that where I am there ye may be also." This promise is as precious to Christ as it ever can be to us. The joy of meeting is surely no less for the coming bridegroom than for the waiting bride. The life of Christ in glory is one of longing expectation: the full glory only comes when His beloved are with Him.

The believer who abides closely in Christ will share with Him in this spirit of expectation. Not so much for the increase of personal happiness, but from the spirit of enthusiastic allegiance to his King, he longs to see Him come in His glory, reigning over every enemy, the fill revelation of God's everlasting love. "Till He come," is the watchword of every true-hearted believer. "Christ shall appear, and we shall appear with Him in glory."

There may be very serious differences in the exposition of the promises of His coming. To one it is plain as day that He is coming very speedily in person to reign on earth, and that speedy coming is his hope and his stay. To another, loving his Bible and his Saviour not less, the coming can mean nothing but the judgment day—the solemn transition from time to eternity, the close of history on earth, the beginning of heaven; and the thought of that manifestation of his Saviour's glory is no less his joy and his strength. It is Jesus, Jesus coming again, Jesus taking us to Himself, Jesus adored as Lord of all, that is to the whole Church the sum and the centre of its hope.

It is by abiding in Christ the Glorified One that the believer will be quickened to that truly spiritual looking for His coming, which alone brings true blessing to the soul. There is an interest in the study of the things which are to be, in which the discipleship of a school is often more marked than the discipleship of Christ the meek; in which contendings for opinions and condemnation of brethren are more striking than any signs of the coming glory. It is only the humility that is willing to learn from those who may have other gifts and deeper revelations of the truth than we, and the love that always speaks gently and tenderly of those who see not as we do, and the heavenliness that shows that the Coming One is indeed already our life, that will persuade either the Church or the world that this our faith is not in the wisdom of men, but in the power of God. To testify of the Saviour as the Coming One, we must be abiding in and bearing the image of Him as the Glorified One. Not the correctness of the views we hold, nor the earnestness with which we advocate them, will prepare us for meeting Him, but only the abiding in Him. Then only can our being manifested in glory with Him be what it is meant to be—a transfiguration, a breaking out and shining forth of the indwelling glory that had been waiting for the day of revelation.

Blessed life! "the life hid with Christ in God," "set in the heavenlies in Christ," abiding in Christ the glorified! Once again the question comes: Can a feeble child of dust really dwell in fellowship with the King of glory? And again the blessed answer has to be given: To maintain that union is the very work for which Christ has all power in heaven and earth at His disposal. The blessing will be given to him who will trust his

Lord for it, who in faith and confident expectation ceases not to yield himself to be wholly one with Him. It was an act of wondrous though simple faith, in which the soul yielded itself at first to the Saviour. That faith grows up to clearer insight and faster hold of God's truth that we are one with Him in His glory. In that same wondrous faith, wondrously simple, but wondrously mighty, the soul learns to abandon itself entirely to the keeping of Christ's almighty power, and the actings of His eternal life. Because it knows that it has the Spirit of God dwelling within to communicate all that Christ is, it no longer looks upon it as a burden or a work, but allows the divine life to have its way, to do its work; its faith is the increasing abandonment of self, the expectation and acceptance of all that the love and the power of the Glorified One can perform. In that faith unbroken fellowship is maintained, and growing conformity realized. As with Moses, the fellowship makes partakers of the glory, and the life begins to shine with a brightness not of this world.

Blessed life! *it is* ours, for Jesus is ours. Blessed life! we have the possession within us in its hidden power, and we have the prospect before us in its fullest glory. May our daily lives be the bright and blessed proof that the hidden power dwells within, preparing us for the glory to be revealed. May our abiding in Christ the Glorified One be our power to live to the glory of the Father, our fitness to share to the glory of the Son.

Andrew Murray
Abide in Christ

> *Seeing that we have a great High Priest who has entered the inmost Heaven, Jesus the Son of God, let us hold firmly to our faith. For we have no superhuman High Priest to whom our weaknesses are unintelligible—he himself has shared fully in all our experience of temptation, except that he never sinned. Let us therefore approach the throne of grace with fullest confidence, that we may receive mercy for our failures and grace to help in the hour of need.*
>
> **Hebrews 4:14-16, Phillips**

"The veil was rent that the way through it might be opened for us; that we might have access to that which is within the veil; that we might enter into a new world, an entirely new way of living in close and intimate fellowship with God. A high priest must have a sanctuary in which he ministers. The mystery of the opened sanctuary is that we can enter too. The inner sanctuary, the Holiest of All, the presence of God, is the sphere of Christ's ministry and our life and service."

Andrew Murray
The Holiest of All

"We are now the free children of God. We may now say to the Law: 'Mister Law, you have lost your throne to Christ. I am free now and a son of God. You cannot curse me any more.' Do not permit the Law to lie in your conscience. Your conscience belongs to Christ. Let Christ be in it and not the Law."

Martin Luther
A Commentary on Galatians

"...think of the dignity and honor which is ours. Sons of God with Him; Heirs of God with Him; one with Him, perfectly identified with the blessed One in God's presence. Therefore He is not ashamed to call us brethren. To walk worthy of the Lord is our calling; and worthy of the Lord we shall walk if we have the great fact of our fellowship with the Son of God as a reality before our souls. It is a sad state to speak theoretically of our position in Christ, to know all this with our intellects and not to manifest it in our lives and show forth the excellencies of Him, who has called us from darkness into his marvellous light. He is not ashamed to call us brethren."

A.C. Gaebelein
The Lord of Glory

"If thou hadst once entered into the mind of Jesus, and hadst tasted yea even a little of his tender love, then wouldst thou care nought for thine own convenience or inconvenience, but wouldst rather rejoice at trouble brought upon thee... He who loveth Jesus, and is inwardly true and free from inordinate affections, is able to turn himself readily unto God, and to rise above himself in spirit, and to enjoy fruitful peace."

Thomas à Kempis
The Imitation of Christ

"I have before me an open door into the mysteries of the Word. I may enter into the deep things of God. Election, Union to Christ, the Second Advent—all these are before me, and I may enjoy them. No promise and no doctrine are now locked up against me. An open door of access is before me in private, and an open door of usefulness in public. God will hear me; God will use me. A door is opened for my onward march to the church above, and for my daily fellowship with saints below. Some may try to shut me up or shut me out, but all in vain."

Charles Spurgeon
Faith's Checkbook

By virtue of the blood of Jesus, you and I, my brothers, may now have courage to enter the holy of holies by way of the one who died and is yet alive, who has made for us a holy means of entry by himself passing through the curtain, that is, his own human nature. Further, since we have a great High Priest set over the household of God, let us draw near with true hearts and fullest confidence, knowing that our inmost souls have been purified by the sprinkling of his blood just as our bodies are cleansed by the washing of clean water. In this confidence let us hold on to the hope that we profess without the slightest hesitation—for he is utterly dependable—and let us think of one another and how we can encourage each other to love and do good deeds.

Hebrews 10:19-24, Phillips

Peace

My Soul, there is a country
Afar beyond the stars,
Where stands a winged sentry
All skillful in the wars;
There, above noise and danger
Sweet Peace sits, crown'd with smiles,
And One born in a manger
Commands the beauteous files.
He is thy gracious friend
And (O my Soul awake!)
Did in pure love descend,
To die here for thy sake.
If thou canst get but thither,
There grows the flow'r of peace,
The rose that cannot wither,
Thy fortress, and thy ease.
Leave then thy foolish ranges,
For none can thee secure,
But One, who never changes,
Thy God, thy life, thy cure.

Henry Vaughan

A Prayer

Jesus, I desire that not a minute of this day would be lived away from your presence. Beckon my heart to yours—even in the midst of my many failures—and teach me to return to you always. Forgive my sins; celebrate with me my triumphs.

May my face be alight with experience of your nearness.

May others see you by simply seeing me today.

In your name, Jesus.

Amen.

The Holy Spirit of Jesus

Touched by Electricity

Charles H. Spurgeon
1855

"And I will pray the Father, and he shall give you another Comforter, that he may abide with you forever; even the Spirit of truth; whom the world cannot receive, because it seeth him not, neither knoweth him: but ye know him; for he dwelleth with you, and shall be in you."

—John 14:16-17

THE INDWELLING OF THE HOLY GHOST is a subject so profound, and so having to do with the inner man, that no soul will be able truly and really to comprehend what I say, unless it has been taught of God. I have heard of an old minister, who told a fellow of one of the Cambridge colleges, that he understood a language that he never learned in all his life. "I have not," he said, "even a smattering of Greek, and I know no Latin, but thank God, I can talk the language of Canaan, and that is more than you can." So, beloved, I shall now have to talk a little of the language of Canaan. If you cannot comprehend me, I am much afraid it is because you are not of Israelitish extraction; you are not a child of God, nor an inheritor of the kingdom of heaven.

We are told in the text, that Jesus would send the Comforter, who would abide in the saints forever; who would dwell with them, and be in them. Old Ignatius, the martyr, used to call himself Theophorus, or Godbearer, "because," said he, "I bear about with me the Holy Ghost." And truly every Christian is a Godbearer. "Know ye not that ye are the temples of the Holy Ghost? for he dwelleth in you?" That man is no Christian who is not the subject of the indwelling of the Holy Spirit; he may talk well, he may understand theology, and be a sound Calvinist; he will be the child of nature finely dressed, but not the living child. He may be a man of so profound an intellect, so gigantic a soul, so comprehensive a mind, and so lofty an imagination, that he may dive into all

The Holy Spirit of Jesus

the secrets of nature, may know the path which the eagle's eye hath not seen, and go into depths where the ken of mortals reacheth not, but he shall not be a Christian with all his knowledge, he shall not be a son of God with all his researches, unless he understands what it is to have the Holy Ghost dwelling in him and abiding in him; yea, and that for ever.

Some people call this fanaticism, and they say, "You are a Quaker; why not follow George Fox?" Well, we would not mind that much: we would follow any one who followed the Holy Ghost. Even he, with all his eccentricities, I doubt not, was, in many cases, actually inspired by the Holy Spirit; and whenever I find a man in whom there rests the Spirit of God, the spirit within me leaps to hear the spirit within him, and we feel that we are one. The Spirit of God in one Christian soul recognizes the Spirit in another. I recollect talking with a good man, as I believe he was, who was insisting that it was impossible for us to know whether we had the Holy Spirit within us or not. I should like him to be here this morning, because I would read this verse to him, "But ye know him, for he dwelleth with you, and shall be in you." Ah! you think you cannot tell whether you have the Holy Spirit or not. Can I tell whether I am alive or not? If I were touched by electricity, could I tell whether I was or not? I suppose I should; the shock would be strong enough to make me know where I stood. So, if I have God within me—if I have Deity tabernacling in my breast—if I have God the Holy Ghost resting in my heart, and making a temple of my body, do you think I shall know it? Call it fanaticism if you will, but I trust that there are some of us who know what it is to be always, or generally, under the influence of the Holy Spirit—always in one sense, generally in another. When we have difficulties, we ask the direction of the Holy Ghost. When we do not understand a portion of Holy Scripture, we ask God the Holy Ghost to shine upon us. When we are depressed, the Holy Ghost comforts us. You cannot tell what the wondrous power of the indwelling of the Holy Ghost is; how it pulls back the hand of the saint when he would touch the forbidden thing; how it prompts him to make a covenant with his eyes; how it binds his feet, lest they should fall in a slippery way; how it restrains his heart, and keeps him from temptation. O ye, who know nothing of the indwelling of the Holy Ghost, despise it not. O despise not the Holy Ghost, for it is the unpardonable sin. "He that speaketh a word against the Son of Man, it shall be forgiven him, but he that speaketh against the Holy Ghost, it shall never be forgiven him, either in this life, or that which is to come." So saith the Word of God. Therefore tremble, lest in anything ye despise the influences of the Holy Spirit.

But before closing this point, there is one little word that pleases me very much, that is "forever." You knew I should not miss that; you were certain I could not let it go without observation. "Abide with you forever."... Ah! blessed be God we can read it—"He shall abide with you forever." Once give me the Holy Ghost, and I shall never lose him till "forever" has run out; till eternity has spun its everlasting rounds...

And now, beloved, it says, "He dwelleth with you, and shall be in you." We will close up with that sweet recollection—the Holy Ghost dwells in all believers and shall be with them... Saints of the Lord! ye have this morning heard that God the Holy Ghost is a person; ye have had it proved to your souls. What follows from this? Why, it followeth how earnest ye should be in prayer to the Holy Spirit, as well as for the Holy Spirit. Let me say that this is an inference that you should lift up your prayers to the Holy Ghost: that you should cry earnestly unto him; for he is able to do exceeding abundantly above all you can speak or think. See this mass of people. What is to convert it? See this crowd? Who is to make my influence permeate through the mass?... Only by incessant prayer for the Holy Spirit; by constantly calling down the influence of the Holy Ghost upon us; we want him to rest upon every page that is printed, and upon every word that is uttered. Let us then be doubly earnest in pleading with the Holy Ghost, that he would come and own our labors; that the whole church at large may be revived thereby, and not ourselves only, but the whole world share in the benefit.

Charles H. Spurgeon
"The Personality of the Holy Ghost"
January 21, 1855

If you really love me, you will keep the commandments I have given you and I shall ask the Father to give you someone else to stand by you, to be with you always. I mean the Spirit of truth, whom the world cannot accept, for it can neither see nor recognise that Spirit. But you recognise him, for he is with you now and will be in your hearts. I am not going to leave you alone in the world—I am coming to you. In a very little while, the world will see me no more but you will see me, because I am really alive and you will be alive too. When that day come, you will realise that I am in my Father, that you are in me, and I am in you... I have said all this while I am still with you. But the one who is coming to stand by you, the Holy Spirit whom the Father will send in my name, will be your teacher and will bring to your minds all that I have said to you. I leave behind with you—peace; I give you my own peace and my gift is nothing like the peace of this world. You must not be distressed and you must not be daunted.

JOHN 14:15-20, 25-27, Phillips

"What Christ did leave, was infinitely more than a reorganisation of Society or a scheme for the reformation of men. On that day of Pentecost a new faculty—that of communing with God's Spirit—came to the birth. And a new force—that of living religion—sprang into existence as a fresh agent in the affairs of the world—a force which Emperors and sacerdotal castes and schools of philosophers had soon to reckon with."

Henry Latham
Pastor Pastorum

"Out of that Upper Room which had been the place of fears they burst with the glad Good News. They smiled at poverty, rejoiced under stripes, were elated at their humiliations, sang in midnight prisons, courted death and shared with every man, everywhere, their own abundant life. God had matched them against that need and they were spiritually adequate. I see nothing, absolutely nothing, that will get the church of today out from behind closed doors except it be this one thing—Pentecost. Increase the ornateness of its ritual as you will, improve the quality and quantity of its religious education as you may, raise the standards of qualifications of the ministry as high as you can, pour money without stint into the coffers of the church—give it everything—everything except this one thing that Pentecost gave, and you are merely ornamenting the dead. Until this sacred Fact takes place, preaching is only lecturing, praying is only repeating formulas, services cease to be service—it all remains earth-bound, circumscribed, inadequate, dead."

E. Stanley Jones
The Christ of Every Road

"...Earnest believers preserve and perpetuate the Church from age to age. The secret of their strength is, that they, by the guidance of the Spirit, found the King's highway up the summit of Christian holiness. They strove, they agonized to plant their feet on that sunlit height. They have left the first principles of the doctrine of Christ, and have gone on to perfection...."

Daniel Steele
Love Enthroned

...here is the staggering thing—that in all which will one day belong to him we have been promised a share (since we were long ago destined for this by the one who achieves his purposes by his sovereign will), so that we, as the first to put our confidence in Christ, may bring praise to his glory! And you too trusted him, when you heard the message of truth, the Gospel of your salvation. And after you gave your confidence to him you were, so to speak, stamped with the promised Holy Spirit as a guarantee of purchase, until the day when God completes the redemption of what he has paid for as his own; and that will again be to the praise of his glory.

Ephesians 1:11-14, Phillips

"There is nothing which is hid from the Lord, but our very secrets are near to Him. Let us therefore do all things as those who have Him dwelling in us, that we may be His temples, and He may be in us as God. Let Christ speak in us, even as He did in Paul. Let the Holy Spirit teach us to speak the things of Christ in like manner as He did."

Ignatius of Antioch
Epistle to the Ephesians

"The history of the Gospel is chiefly the history of Christ's conquest over the spirit of the world. And the number of true Christians is only the number of those who, following the Spirit of Christ, have lived contrary to this spirit of the world.

"'If any man hath not the Spirit of Christ, he is none of His.' Again, 'Whatsoever is born of God, overcometh the world.' 'Set your affection on things above, and not on things on the earth; for ye are dead, and your life is hid with Christ in God.' [Rom. viii. 9.; 1 John v. 4.; Col. iii. 2, 3] This is the language of the whole New Testament: this is the mark of Christianity: you are to be dead, that is, dead to the spirit and temper of the world, and live a new life in the Spirit of Jesus Christ."

William Law
A Serious Call to a Devout and Holy Life

"For most of my years I have spoken about the eternal life as the 'afterlife,' as 'life after death.' But the older I become, the less interest my 'afterlife' holds for me. Worrying not only about tomorrow, next year, and the next decade, but even about the next life seems a false preoccupation. Wondering how things will be for me after I die seems, for the most part, a distraction. When my clear goal is the eternal life, that life must be reachable right now, where I am, because eternal life is life in and with God, and God is where I am here and now.

"The great mystery of the spiritual life—the life in God—is that we don't have to wait for it as something that will happen later. Jesus says: 'Dwell in me as I dwell in you.' It is this divine in-dwelling that is eternal life. It is the active presence of God at the center of my living—the movement of God's Spirit within us—that gives us the eternal life."

Henri Nouwen
Here and Now

God's Grandeur

The world is charged with the grandeur of God.
It will flame out, like shining from shook foil;
It gathers to a greatness, like the ooze of oil
Crushed. Why do men then now not reck his rod?
Generations have trod, have trod, have trod;
And all is seared with trade; bleared, smeared with toil,
And wears man's smudge and shares man's smell; the soil
Is bare now, nor can foot feel, being shod.
And for all this, nature is never spent;
There lives the dearest freshness deep down things;
And though the last lights off the black West went,
Oh, morning, at the brown brink eastward, springs—
Because the Holy Ghost over the bent
World broods with warm breast and with ah! bright wings.

Gerard Manley Hopkins

A Prayer

Jesus, there can never be enough of you in my life, and, also, there is simply too little. I want to know you more and to experience your personal presence. I want your alive life to live in me; I want to see the works of your power streaming forth from me.

O Lord Jesus, would you allow me more of your Spirit? Would you flood my inner life like you did your first disciples? You have already set me free and stamped my heart with your Holy Spirit: I desire now to be filled to the full!

Thank you that you hear my every prayer.

I only want more of you.

In your name, Jesus.

Amen.

The Holy Spirit of Jesus

Extending the Realm of the Kingdom of Heaven

The Fresh Air of Heaven

J.B. Phillips
1956

THE TOTAL IMPRESSION of the close study of the Gospels is an indelible conviction that the well-nigh incredible has happened—that the Creator has visited this world in human form. He brings with Him confirmation of our highest hopes, He endorses our finest longings, and He confirms many of our intuitions. But of course He does far more than this. First, He introduces a new kind of truth—a kind of "supersense" which transcends our earthly viewpoint. We may find sometimes our values disconcertingly reversed, sometimes we find we have been looking at things from the wrong angle. Now that we have this revelation of truth, there is no need to grope or fumble. We have certain basic truths unquestionably revealed. We have a standard by which our scale of values and our conscience may be adjusted. It is not that all our questions are immediately answered. It is not that everything becomes immediately plain and that there are no more mysteries. But it is true that we now have enough light by which to live; we see something at least of life's point and purpose, and we know where we are going. What is more, the humble and obedient are guaranteed an active, energetic, contemporary Spirit of Truth. In other words, although we see the Character of God focused historically in the time and space set-up, we come to see and know that that human appearance is only the outcrop of what is eternally true. (That is why the material on which a New Testament translator works is alive under his hands.) It is almost too good to be true, but it is true that the One Who walked and talked in the countryside, the streets and houses of Palestine nearly two thousand years ago, is in every way as alive and active in the world of today.

The second important revelation which God-become-Man gave us, and which indeed His Spirit is continually prepared to endorse, is that this little life is lived against a background, at present invisible, of timeless Reality. Some men have always felt that this must be so, since man's longings and intuitions, as well as his sense of justice, go far beyond the limits of life in this present temporary existence. To put it in another way, there is another dimension to life altogether, the dimension of "eternity." This present life is interpenetrated by the Real World far more than we know. For most of us it is only very occasionally that we get our flashes of conviction, and it is of immeasurable comfort to know, on the authority of that Personal Visit, that our feeble intuition was right and that this short, earthly life, important and significant though it may be in its setting, is no more than a prelude to a share in the timeless Life of God.

All this and much more floods our minds as we study afresh the four Gospel records. But this wonderful quality of living, this drawing on unseen spiritual resources, this plunging of the sharp sword of truth into the muddle of human sins and stupidities, might have ended with the crucifixion of Jesus. If it had, we should indeed have been left something, for every true seer and poet and philosopher has left us the richer. But the special glory of the New Testament is that we are not merely shown a shining beacon of one perfect human life but we are told of what happened after that human life was ended. The light persists, the power continues, the wind of Heaven does not cease to blow. If you will not misunderstand me, in one sense I have been even more thrilled as a translator to come into contact with the highly-charged material of the Acts and the Epistles than I was when translating the Gospels. For if God really became Man, the light and power and splendour of the Gospel-story is only to be expected. But to find that this was not merely a single unique demonstration but the beginning of a new way of living, the founding of a new Kingdom and of a new fellowship, is exciting indeed!

Consequently, the close study of the book commonly called the Acts of the Apostles proved an exhilaration. The ideas and ideals of God-become-Man take shape and form: the glory has not departed, it continues and expands. For the first time in human history we are seeing a group of men and women united in devotion to the unseen King, joined in an unconquerable fellowship. We may be reasonably certain that Luke was a most careful historian and was not prone to exaggeration. Yet we find his story of the Young Church in action bearing the same stamp of supra-human quality as we find in the Gospels. The sick are not merely prayed about, they are healed, often suddenly and dramatically. Mental and psychological diseases ("possession by evil spirits," in the jargon of those days) proved equally susceptible to the new power in the Church. Perhaps, above all, that miracle which is theoretically unattainable is performed again and again—human nature is changed. The fresh air of Heaven blows gustily through these pages, and the sense that ordinary human life is continually open to the Spirit of God is very marked. There is not yet a dead hand of tradition; there is no over-organisation to stifle initiative; there is neither security nor complacency to destroy sensitivity to the living God. The early Church lived dangerously, but never before has such a handful of people exerted such widespread influence. There is a courage to match the vision; there is a flexible willingness to match the divine leadership. And there is that unshakable certainty against which persecution, imprisonment, and death prove quite powerless. To put it shortly and in the common phrase, the lasting excitement which follows the reading of this book is this: the thing works! What might have remained no more than a beautiful ideal is set to work in an actual human situation, and with truly astonishing impetus the Church moves forward on its way.

All this is without doubt exciting enough, but from the point of view of Christian evidence the best is yet to be. For, after all, it might be argued, and indeed has been argued, that the Man Jesus did exist, but that some years after His death, perhaps after a generation or so, His followers wrote romantic and idealistic accounts of His life. Again, it is possible to argue that Luke's second book, the Acts of the Apostles, is something of an idealisation of the beginnings of the Christian Church. But even if these contentions are true, if both the Gospels and the Acts were propaganda for the Christian sect and therefore not to be wholly relied upon as unbiased history, the critics of Christianity have still to explain the incontrovertible evidence of the "Epistles" or Letters. With one or two minor exceptions, these are universally accepted as authentic, and it seems to me that Christians today do not always realise how valuable they are as evidence for the proof of the Faith. For here we have no self-conscious documents, but vivid human letters, often bearing strong evidence of the emotion under which they were written. There is some case to be made out for arguing that the four evangelists knew what they were doing—they were writing lives of Jesus Christ to be read among Christians and possibly non-Christians. Although they could not have foreseen the vast weight of authority that would later be accorded to their words, they may well have known that they were in a sense writing "holy Scripture." But this is not true of Paul, for example, at all. For the most part he wrote to certain groups of Christians in certain circumstances, and he had no idea that he was writing holy Scripture at the time. In translating his letters, it is not difficult to picture that solitary, courageous figure, writing or dictating his letters in great haste and urgency. Sometimes he was in prison, sometimes he was in poor health, frequently he was torn with anxiety for his new-born converts. He wrote to meet the needs of those for whom he was writing, completely unconscious that in years to come millions of people would study his every word with the deepest attention. Yet the inspiration of his words, which I believe to be largely unconscious, strikes us forcibly today. He had no idea, certainly, that he was composing Christian evidence! Yet the life reflected, as well as expressed, in the pages of his unselfconscious letters is plainly of the supra-human quality.

Now, if we were to compile a history of any place or nation, one of our most valuable discoveries would be a packet of letters reflecting the life of a certain part of that history. Newspapers, broadsheets, pamphlets, and any other printed matter would have their value, of course; but because they were written for the public eye and probably to prove a particular point, we should be very wary of accepting them as unbiased evidence. But that would not be true of a bundle of private letters simply because they were not being written for the public at all and the writer had no particular axe to grind. They would, in all probability, reflect most accurately the customs, habits, and thoughts of the times in which they were written. Now, if this is true in the field of purely secular history, it is just as true, though of far deeper significance, when we study historically the beginnings of Christianity. It is what the Letters say and what the Letters imply, it is the new-quality life revealed by these human unselfconscious documents, which gives us, to my mind, our most valuable Christian evidence. What impression is left upon our minds, or, if I may again be personal, what impression is left upon my mind after spending some years in translating these letters? Above all, I think, that men and women are being changed: the timid become brave, the filthy-minded become pure in heart, the mean and selfish become loving and generous. It is quite plain that the writers of these letters took it as a matter of course, as a matter of observed experience, that if men and women were open to the Spirit of God, then they could be and were transformed. The resources of God are not referred to as vague pieties but as readily available spiritual power. Quite clearly a positive torrent of love and wisdom, sanity and courage, has already flooded human life, and is always ready to flow wherever human hearts are open.

Now, critics of Christianity have somehow got to explain this if they are to have a leg to stand on. Let them read these Letters for themselves, and attempt to explain these transformations of character. No one had anything to gain in those days from being a Christian; indeed, there was a strong chance that the Christian would lose security and property, and even life itself. Yet, reflected in the pages of these Letters, both men and women are exhibiting superb courage and are growing, as naturally as fruit upon a tree, those qualities of the spirit of which the world is so lamentably short. To my mind we are forced to the conclusion that something is at work here far above and beyond normal human experience, which can only be explained if we accept what the New Testament itself claims; that is, that ordinary men and women had become, through the power of Christ, sons and daughters of God.

J.B. Phillips
New Testament Christianity

> *Then those who welcomed* [Peter's Pentecost] *message were baptised, and on that day alone about three thousand souls were added to the number of disciples. They continued steadily learning the teaching of the apostles, and joined in their fellowship, in the breaking of bread, and in prayer. Everyone felt a deep sense of awe, while many miracles and signs took place through the apostles. All the believers shared everything in common; they sold their possessions and goods and divided the proceeds among the fellowship according to individual need. Day after day they met by common consent in the Temple; they broke bread together in their homes, sharing meals with simple joy. They praised God continually and all the people respected them. Every day the Lord added to their number those who were finding salvation.*

Acts 2:41-47, Phillips

"Jesus Christ came to restore the kingdom of God upon earth. He came not simply to offer salvation to every individual man. It was his design to found a holy community, from which, as from a new humanity reconstituted by him, filled with his Spirit and living by his life, the Gospel should go forth into all the world."

Edmund de Pressensé
The Early Years of Christianity

"God's promise is, that He will work in us to will as well as to do of His good pleasure. This, of course, means that He will take possession of our will, and work it for us, and that His suggestions will come to us, not so much commands from the outside, as desires springing up within. They will originate in our will; we shall feel as though we wanted to do so and so, not as though we must. And this makes it a service of perfect liberty; for it is always easy to do what we desire to do, let the accompanying circumstances be as difficult as they may."

Hannah Whitall Smith
The Christian's Secret of a Happy Life

"Paul's conception of a Christian community is a body of which the Spirit of Christ is the soul. The individual members are all full of the Spirit, and their individual powers and capacities are laid hold of, vivified, and strengthened by the indwelling Spirit in such a way that each is 'gifted' and enabled to do some special service for Christ and for His Church in the society in which he is placed. Every true Christian is 'gifted' in this way. In this respect all are equal and of the same spiritual rank. The equality, however, is neither monotonous nor mechanical. Men have different natural endowments, and these lead to a diversity of 'gifts,' all of which are serviceable in their places, and enable the separate members to perform different services, useful and necessary, for the spiritual life of the whole community and for the growth in sanctification of every member."

Thomas M. Lindsey
The Church and the Ministry in the Early Centuries

"The true inwardness of the Church is reflected, not in the Temple, which Christ said could be destroyed without loss, and not in the synagogue, which He seems to have abandoned with deliberate decision, but in the sending out of the Seventy. The Church is intended as a concrete answer to the prayer that laborers be sent forth to the harvest. The Company of Jesus is not people streaming to a shrine; and it is not people making up an audience for a speaker; it is laborers engaged in the harvesting task of reaching their perplexed and seeking brethren with something so vital that, if it is received, it will change their lives."

Elton Trueblood
The Company of the Committed

"It was as a Bridegroom Christ came, anointed with all the perfumes of a dedicated love, and until the last bitter hour of His rejection, He moved with such lyric joyousness across the earth, that life became festive in His presence. It is as a Bride the church exists on earth, and if no festive smiles are awakened by its presence, and no gracious unsealing of the founts of love in human hearts, then is it not Christ's Church, for He has passed elsewhere with another company to the marriage-feast, and His Church stands without, before a barred and darkened door."

W.J. Dawson
The Empire of Love

"St. John lived to about the age of a hundred. He was at last so weak that he could not walk into the church; so he was carried in, and used to say continually to his people, 'Little children, love one another.' Some of them, after a time, began to be tired of hearing this, and asked him why he repeated the words so often, and said nothing else to them. The Apostle answered, 'Because it is the Lord's commandment, and if this be done it is enough.'"

J.C. Robertson
Sketches of Church History

"We have a chance to prove our glorious God, to prove that His joy is strength and that His peace passeth all understanding, and to know the love of Christ that passeth knowledge."

Amy Carmichael
Edges of His Ways

Blessed Assurance

Blessed assurance, Jesus is mine!
O what a foretaste of glory divine!
Heir of salvation, purchase of God,
Born of His Spirit, washed in His blood!

Chorus:
This is my story, this is my song,
Praising my Saviour all the day long.

Perfect submission, perfect delight,
Visions of rapture now burst on my sight;
Angels descending bring from above
Echoes of mercy, whispers of love.

Perfect submission, all is at rest,
I in my Saviour am happy and blest,—
Watching and waiting, looking above,
Filled with His goodness, lost in His love.

Frances Jane Crosby VanAlstyne

A Prayer

Jesus, I present my life as an offering for your purposes, as a vessel for your Spirit, as a place where you may extend the Kingdom of Heaven. I want my every day to be awake to your voice and leading. I want my lifetime's work to be just like yours: loving the Father, loving others, showing forth your magnificence.

Oh, use me, Lord! Make of me a saint of yours! Allow me to experience you every single day!

I want to do the very things you're doing—and did!

I want to reflect your face to all I see!

I love you.

In your name, Jesus.

Amen.

Afterword

G.K. Chesterton
1925

TO SUM UP: the sanity of the world was restored and the soul of man offered salvation by something which did indeed satisfy the two warring tendencies of the past; which had never been satisfied in full and most certainly never satisfied together. It met the mythological search for romance by being a story and the philosophical search for truth by being a true story. That is why the ideal figure had to be a historical character, as nobody had ever felt Adonis or Pan to be a historical character. But that is also why the historical character had to be the ideal figure; and even fulfil many of the functions given to these other ideal figures; why he was at once the sacrifice and the feast, why he could be shown under the emblems of the growing vine or the rising sun. The more deeply we think of the matter the more we shall conclude that, if there be indeed a God, his creation could hardly have reached any other culmination than this granting of a real romance to the world. Otherwise the two sides of the human mind could never have touched at all; and the brain of man would have remained cloven and double; one lobe of it dreaming impossible dreams and the other repeating invariable calculations. The picture-makers would have remained forever painting the portrait of nobody. The sages would have remained forever adding up numerals that came to nothing. It was that abyss that nothing but an incarnation could cover; a divine embodiment of our dreams; and he stands above that chasm whose name is more than priest and older even than Christendom; Pontifex Maximus, the mightiest maker of a bridge...

It is one among many stories; only it happens to be a true story. It is one among many philosophies; only it happens to be the truth.

We accept it; and the ground is solid under our feet and the road is open before us. It does not imprison us in a dream of destiny or a consciousness of the universal delusion. It opens to us not only incredible heavens, but what seems to some an equally incredible earth, and makes it credible. This is the sort of truth that is hard to explain because it is a fact; but it is a fact to which we can call witnesses. We are Christians and Catholics not because we worship a key, but because we have passed a door; and felt the wind that is the trumpet of liberty blow over the land of the living.

G.K. Chesterton
The Everlasting Man

ABOUT
SEA HARP PRESS

Sea Harp is a specialty press with one overarching aim: in the words of Andrew Murray, to "be much occupied with Jesus, and believe much in Him, as the True Vine." Our mission is twofold: to reinvigorate the Church's reading of the best of the past, and to bring out fresh editions of both today's and tomorrow's classics — all for the purpose of personal encounter with Jesus Himself.

For every piece of media we consider publishing, we ask two fundamental questions:

- Is this work entirely about the person of Jesus of Nazareth?
- Would the Early Church have thought this work worthy of sharing?

We take our name from the original Hebrew word for the Sea of Galilee—*Kinneret*: כִּנֶּרֶת: meaning "harp"—which was given because of the harp-like shape of the shoreline around which Jesus ministered. It was, in less words, a place known as the Harp-Sea.

Thank you for joining us as we walk the Way with that most wonderful Man of Galilee.

the
SEA *of*
GALILEE

WWW.SEAHARP.COM

Made in the USA
Monee, IL
03 May 2026

49437441R00059